MYSTERY OF THE TREES

Native American Markers of a Cultural Way of Life that Soon may be Gone

Don and Diane Wells

With

Dr. John Nardo, Robert Wells and Lamar Marshall

This book is available from the publisher:

Mountain Stewards Publishing Co.
P. O. Box 1525
Jasper, GA 30143
www.mountainstewards.org
email: sales@mountainstewards.org
Telephone: 706-692-1565

Contents

This book is dedicated to our Indian brethren who, at the
hands of our forefathers, lost their home lands, their kinfolk,
their culture, and most importantly,
part of their pride and dignity.
No apology, however sincere, can compensate for their loss.

-The Authors

PREFACE

Introduction

Elaine Jordan of Ellijay, GA introduced the nation, on a larger scale, to the subject of Indian Trail Trees in her book published in 1997. Although a lot had been written about the trees prior to Elaine's book, little of it has seen the light of day in the 21st Century. Elaine's little book was the "day-star" that led many across the nation to consider this part of tribal culture that had been hidden below the radar for years. In fact, the knowledge of the existence these trees, their use and their being a part of the Indian culture was not well know to some tribal elders since this aspect of tribal culture had been all but lost.

In early 2007, a group of people from four states met at Hobbs State Park in northwest Arkansas to share information about their findings on researching Indian Trail Trees. Prior to that meeting, the authors had only considered that bent trees existed mostly on the southeastern part of the United States. All who attended that meeting agreed that there was a wider distribution of oddly shaped trees and that bending of these trees was obviously due to many Native American Tribes.

The group decided in 2007 to form a collaborative effort to research the trees on an expanded scale and to create the Trail Tree Project as a nationwide effort. The Mountain Stewards, a non-profit, 501(c)(3) organization located in Jasper, GA was selected to manage the effort and to maintain the databases of the groups' information. The size of the group of researchers quickly grew as more people signed on to assist in other different states.

Over the period of 2007 to 2009, the Trail Tree Project was expanded to include the development of a documentary on the trees called the Mystery of the Trees and the mapping of Indian Trails. The Mapping of Indian Trails grew out of the fact that some of the bent trees were found marking the old Indian trails. The trees lead to trails and trails led to the trees.

In late 2007, the Mountain Stewards Trail Tree Project Team met with Lamar Marshall of WildSouth and Gail King of Southeastern Anthropological Institute to learn about the work they had done on locating the Benge Trail of Tears Route in Alabama. That meeting led to an effort to develop more efficient techniques and software for mapping old trails by using Geographic Information Systems Technology, GPS Navigational tools, topographic earth models and imagery such as found on Google Earth.

Dr. John Nardo, a physician by profession but a consummate software programmer by avocation, began the task of developing the software programs and integrating off-the-shelf software with powerful computer processors to handle large data sets that were in the gigabyte range. Eventually, he built a new computer with four dual processors and a terabyte of data storage in order to handle the data processing task. Throughout 2008, the data processing techniques were refined and improved to a point where most 1700-1800 survey maps can now be geo-registered and the Indian trails data extracted.

Today, trail data is being extracted from the maps and placed on topographic maps and the trails ground-truthed through a "boots-on-the-ground" technique to validate that the trail is actually where it was thought to exist.

Throughout the 20th Century, a lot had been written about the Indian Trail Trees but without the Internet connectivity of today, few were exposed to the subject.

Knowledge about the trees seemed to grow in volume for a few years and then wane. With each new decade, new persons picked up the cause and pursued an effort to get the knowledge about the trees documented. But as each author died, the subject began to slide back down below the radar until a new person with a passion for the subject came on the scene.

The purpose of this book is to finally document the collective data and knowledge accumulated over the past few hundred years so that a more permanent record of this aspect of Native American culture is not lost again. Elaine Jordan died in 2009 and with her death, the publishing of her book probably ended.

Elaine's book provided documentation of some of the bent tree shapes. But there are many more which we will offer to show the collective knowledge that exists today.

Across the United States and Canada, the oddly shaped trees are known by different names. These names include, but are not limited to, Bent Tree, Trail Tree, Thong Tree, Yoke Tree, Signal Tree, Indian Tree, Marker Tree and many more. Out west where the trees were used to support the Indians way of life including food, they are called Peeled Trees, Medicine Tree, Culturally Modified Trees and Bent Trees. Some trees were not bent by the Indians but rather had carved symbols on smooth-skinned trees such as beech trees. These trees are called Witness Trees, Dedroglyth Trees or Arborglyth Trees.

In the 1960-1970's. Laura Hubler of Ironton, Missouri with the help of a few others searched for the bent trees in MO, AR, KS and a few other states. But there was no GPS to document the trees location and mapping technology was limited. Thus most of the trees that Laura found will have to be located again. Elaine Jordan searched and documented the trees in a few northern Georgia counties but she did not have GPS either and the location of most of those trees is also lost.

In the last decade, the Internet has opened the information channels and connectivity to millions. And the military has released the GPS technology to the public so that we can all determine where we are on the earth to within a few feet. With this information technology at out finger tips, trees can be located by anyone and reported to the Trail Tree Project. Since setting up the reporting system for the Trail Trees on the Mountain Stewards web site, the data on the tree locations has been pouring in from across the nation. As more data is received, more becomes known about this cultural aspect of tribal life.

The Trail Tree Project is a "work in progress." Since the Indians have been removed from their home lands for almost 200 years, many of the trees are approaching the end of their normal life. Disease, storm damages, development and willful destruction has taken its toll on the trees that are left. There are fewer trees to find each year and yet, almost each day brings a new discovery. With time, the trees will be found and the accumulated evidence will allow the National Historical Preservation laws to be changed to preserve this part of Native American history.

Writing any book takes a lot of research. In today's world of the Internet, research has gotten easier than in the past when one had to travel to many different places to locate sources of information. There is still a lot of travel but it is less of a problem. One aspect of doing research has been vastly improved due to the generosity of Google.

Google several years ago made the corporate commitment to locate archival sources of information that had historical value and began digitizing these documents. They then put them on the Google Books web site so that all would have the opportunity to study these long forgotten historical sources. Without their magnanimous support for research, it would be near to impossible to have written this book.

As mentioned earlier, this book is a "work in progress." The publishing of the book will lock in what information we have at that moment in time. But the day we publish the book, we will learn more information. In the future hopefully, we will be able to publish a sequal book that will contain any new information learned about this cultural aspect of the Indian way of life.

Chapter 1

NATIVE AMERICAN CULTURE AND TREES

Trees were always an important part of the Indian way of life. The fruit of the trees provided food, and for some tribes, both in the east and west, harvesting the cambium layer of the tree was a source of food and medicine. The bark of some trees was used for medicine, for making dyes and for baskets. Parts of the trees were harvested for making canoes, utensils, bows, cradleboards and more.

Native Americans contend that trees, plants, animals, and people all have a place in the circle of life. All living things, great or small, are an important part of the universe. The Indians believe all living things have a spiritual being. The Indians would offer up prayers for forgiveness before they would take the life of any living thing including a tree.

Kerry Holton, Chief of the Delaware Nation, said in an interview that "trees were spiritual to the Indians." The Delaware (Lenape) Indians would carve a mask in a tree called a Mesingw and then harvest that tree to be part of their ceremonial structure.

Most tribes had a particular species of tree with which they identified as being a part of their culture. In 2004, the Osage Nation was invited to participate in the Bicentennial Ceremony of the Lewis and Clark Expedition in St. Louis, MO. The Osage planted an Osage orange tree inside a red oak destroyed by lightning. Eddy Red Eagle of the Osage Nation said, "Red Oak was Osage." it's the tree they believe best typifies the Osage Indians.

The cedar tree is sacred to many Indians. It is not uncommon to find boughs of cedar hanging in a North American Indian home. In fact, many believe the red cedar to be the *tree of life*. Western red cedar has been called *the cornerstone of north-*

west coast Indian culture. Many parts of the cedar tree were used to support their way of life. White cedar was important to the way of life of the Chippewa, Potawatomi, Penobscot, Cree, Menominee and Iroquois Indians. Some trees marked places of great importance to the Indians such as places where treaties were signed or where the chiefs of many tribes met to discuss tribal business. One of those trees was the Shackamaxon Elm Tree. Shackamaxon means where the chiefs meet. It was under that tree where the Lenape and William Penn signed the first treaty between the colonists and the Indians in 1682. Kerry Holton said, "The tree was so important that the British built a fort near it during the Revolutionary War and posted guards to protect it[1]." The tree died in 1810 when a storm blew it down.

Other important trees were known as council or treaty trees. The tree in Figure 1-1 is located in Dardanelle City Park in Arkansas. It is the site where a major treaty was signed between the Cherokees and the Arkansas Territorial Government in 1820. That tree still stands today almost 200 years later.

Figure 1-1 Dardanelle Treaty Oak Tree

Since trees were a very important part of the Indian way of life, it is likely to assume that trees played an important role in Indian travel. One of the most famous trees used by Indians in their travels is known today as the Signal or Candelabrum Tree located in the Cascade Valley Park near Akron, Ohio. This over-300-year-old burr oak tree is believed to have marked a place where the Indians portaged their canoes between two large water routes. After the Indians were removed from this area, pioneers used the same tree to mark the place to portage canoes. It is uncertain whether the tree was bent naturally or by the Indians, but the fact that it was used to mark a place to portage canoes seems to indicate some human intervention in its shape.

Figure 1-2 Camdelabrum Tree Near Akron, Ohio

Historical accounts of the first explorers of the North American continent documented their travels across large segments of the continent. These explorers didn't have to do a lot of trail blazing. They followed existing trails laid out by the Indians. This interconnecting trail system allowed the Indians to go short or even great distances for tribal gatherings, for hunting, for trading and for war. The early explorers used these same trails to search for gold which they believed the Indian possessed.

These trails were so extensive that surely there had to be a system of marking the trails so that you could find your way to a particular location. Thus, bending trees to mark trails and places of importance would be a natural use of the living thing important to the Indian way of life. Places of importance can include shelter areas, water sources, medicinal gathering sites, grave sites and more. Bending trees or using slashes on trees was undoubtedly the primary trail markers used. Where there were few trees, the Indians used rock cairns and other objects to indicate the pathways. While the Indians could follow these signs, most of the early explorers had to use Indian guides to help them to their destination.

In the chapters to follow, the evidence to support the existence of the bent trees, why knowledge about this cultural aspect of Indian life has seemingly been lost and the various configurations of the trees located will be delineated.

Chapter 2

EVIDENCE SUPPORTING THE EXISTENCE OF INDIAN TRAIL TREES

Some historians are quick to point out that there are no historical accounts written by anthropologists or academicians of note that document the existence of the bent trees and their use. In particular, James Mooney's extensive writings[2] about living with the Cherokees for many years do not mention the bent trees. The historians believe he would have been told about them or his observations would have noted their existence. However, Mooney's time with the Cherokees was in the late 1890s long after the Cherokee culture had been affected by the white man's way, and the use of trees to mark trails and other places of importance may have already disappeared and its knowledge been forgotten.

Joining the historians are some of those with training in forestry and other educational backgrounds involving nature studies. Their training did not cover the possibility of human intervention in the shaping of trees. In fact, many will vocally defend their opinion that any tree bent in a funny shape was caused by natural occurrences. Yet, the knowledge of shaping bonsai trees had existed for hundreds if not thousands of years, and today, arborsculpturists can create almost any shape in a living tree imaginable.

There are others who don't believe the Indians were intelligent enough to have figured out how to manipulate the shape of a tree so that it could be used for a variety of purposes. But the indigenous peoples of the continent had existed for over 10,000 years, and through their observational powers they had learned the way trees were bent by nature, and they would have known how to duplicate that phenomenon.

This chapter will lay out some of the evidence that has been found in archives, libraries, and other sources in which the existence of the trees was documented by early scholars and writers who observed the bent trees in various parts of the country. The evidence can be grouped into four categories; scientific, historical, interviews with tribal elders and old timers, and the overwhelming accumulation of tree similarities in many states that clearly shows these bent trees were not a natural occurrence.

SCIENTIFIC EVIDENCE

Dendrochronology is the science of studying tree rings to not only reveal very accurately the age of the tree but also to determine the dates of traumatic events during the life of the tree. Drought, ice storms, fires, and other natural events leave indisputable records on the rings of the trees. Archaeologists and foresters have used this technology extensively to age living things. The scientific evidence is based on dendrochronology. A number of bent trees have been cored and the ages of the trees dated to times when only the Indians occupied the area where the trees were found.

Marilyn Martorano, an archaeologist with RMC Consultants, Inc., stated in a filmed interview that "archaeologists use dendrochronology to get a precise date on a tree that has been altered by the Indians because it tells them a lot about the Indians that had lived in the area in the past and about their lifestyle."[3]

Dr. Georgina DeWeese of the University of West Georgia led the effort to core the bent trees in north Georgia and elsewhere to age them as well as to better understand aspects of the tree deformation. Dr. DeWeese in writing her doctorial dissertation cored hundreds of normal oak trees in the Appalachian Mountains. She stated that "it was difficult to age some of these trees precisely because the early years of growth were made up of fat rings (rapid growth). An algorithm had to be developed to estimate the early years of tree age."[4]

When Dr. DeWeese analyzed the bent tree cores, she found a totally different pattern of early tree rings. In fact, these early rings were spaced very close together showing stress in the tree that could be the result of the tree having been bent at a very early (sapling) age.

Trees of different bent shape characteristics were chosen to be cored. In north Georgia, where there are many bent trees remaining and where these trees are suspected of marking old Indian Trails, twenty-two trees were cored. The majority of trees cored were white oak as this was the primary species of tree used by the southeastern Indians.

The oldest tree cored was determined to be from around 1776. The exact date could not be determined as the center core of the tree had begun to rot. Oak trees, which can live to about 300 years, die from the center. Thus, many of the trees that may have been bent by Indians before they were removed from the eastern US are approaching the end of their natural life.

The cored trees in north Georgia were dated from 1776-1828 with a number of them in the 1770s to the 1790s. These dates place the trees in the time frame when the Cherokees were the only people living in the area.

In addition to coring bent trees, normal unbent white oak trees were selected near the bent trees and they were cored also. These trees were found to be aged from 1707 to 1816. Some foresters and others claim that there could be no trees that old left in the mountains since all the trees were logged out in the late 1800s and early 1900s. In fact, these trees do exist and they certainly were a part of the life of the Cherokees.

In Colorado, Marilyn Martorano, has been coring some of the peeled or culturally modified ponderosa pines. She has discovered that many of these trees date to the early 1800s. However, one tree that was studied in 2008 was determined to have been peeled by Utes in 1729. The Utes occupied that part of Colorado until 1876.

As more bent trees are cored, more of the scientific truth about these trees will be discovered.

HISTORICAL DOCUMENTATION EVIDENCE – SCIENTIFIC JOURNAL REPORTS, MAGAZINES, NEWS ARTICLES AND MORE

Starting from about 1900, researchers have documented the evidence of the trees and in some cases interviewed tribal elders about them. These articles, while seeming sufficient to document the trees' existence, do not serve as absolute proof to some. Many in the academic community consider the existence of Indian trail trees a preposterous hoax. Since there is no written record of the trees' existence in reports in refereed journals by accredited historians, their existence is discounted. However, when one searches the archives, historical reports, news articles and other sources of information that are available to document the early history of this Native American culture, the evidence of the trees' existence is convincing. The Mountain Stewards have been researching, gathering and studying these sources of information. A database has been developed that not only details the wealth of information that is presently available on this subject but continues to grow as new evidence is found.

Frank Reed Grover (1858-1919) was one of the first authors to write extensively about Indian trails and Indian trees. He was a lawyer by profession, having been admitted to the bar in Illinois in 1883, but he had a passion for history. He was also a prominent member of the Illinois State Historical Society. He lived in Evanston, Illinois, now a suburb of Chicago, which has a rich Indian history. Beginning in early 1900 and extending to his death in 1919, Mr. Grover did research and documented the Indian history of Illinois in major historical writings.

In one of his first reports from 1901, he documented the existence of the Indian trees stating,

> *"There is at various places along the North Shore and following closely the line of the old Indian trails some curious trees, most of them large elms, that apparently have been broken down when saplings by Indians to*

mark the trail; that custom has been followed in oth-
er localities, and it is probable here. The trees are in-
variably large and, if this convenient theory is correct,
this work of so marking the trail must have been done
a century or more ago."[5]

To further document his theory about the trail trees, Grover wrote,

"But some six years ago, there were eleven of these
(trail) trees in perfect alignment, leading from the site
of an old Indian village at Highland Park, Ill, in a
northwesterly direction for several miles, most of them
still standing and can be easily identified, and what is
particularly of interest is the fact that all of these trees
are white oak, while another line of similar trees sup-
posed to mark another trail farther to the south, near
Wilmette, ILL., are without exception white elms."[6]

He continued his research into Indian history and the bent
trees and, with the help of Mr. A. W. Watriss and Mr. C. S.
Raddin of the Evanston Historical Society and Vice-President
of the Chicago Academy of Sciences, documented these trees
with photographs and their locations.[6]

Whether influenced by the work of Frank Grover or others, the interest in the Indian trees blossomed in and around
the small towns of Wilmette, Kenilworth and Winnetka in the
Chicago area from around 1939 to at least 1955. Pictures of
some of the Indian trees located in Wilmette were published
in the *Wilmette Life* newspaper on March 23, 1939.[7]

The *Wilmette Life* news article reported,

"Also at that time there was a deep worn path follow-
ing the line of the lake shore. This was known as the
Green Bay Trail. Most old settlers agreed that it fol-
lowed Clark Street, Chicago, to Rose Hill. there it di-
vided, one part taking the route over Ridge Avenue in
Evanston. The westerly route was used in wet weather,
as it was higher. The two joined just north of the Gross
Point lighthouse and continued over the sand ridge

into Wilmette…There are at various places along the North Shore on several of the old Indian trails, some curious trees. These show that they were bent at right angles when they were young and later grew upright again. They were bent and tied several feet from the ground in the direction of the trail to be followed."[7]

Chief Evergreen, a Potawatomi Indian in the Wilmette, Illinois, area where many Indian Trail Trees did exist in the early 1900s, befriended a local photographer, Raymond Gloede. Chief Evergreen told Raymond Gloede about the Trail trees. He and several other Potawatomi Indians were photographed by a Trail tree. The Chief and other Indians were in full Indian dress. Many local citizens also participated in the picture event. This was reported in the September 23, 1965, issue of the Wilmette newspaper.[10]

Others articles showing pictures of the bent trees in the Chicago area were published in a Chicago newspaper[8], a Wilmette newspaper[9] and other publications to be discussed later in this chapter. Many of these Indian trees are related to the Potawatomi Indians who had extensive trails and village sites along the north shore of the Lake Michigan.

Following closely on the heels of Frank Grover, Katherine Stanley Nickolson wrote a book entitled, *Historic American Trees* published in 1922.[11] Her book quoted some of the work of Frank Grover and added to the data on the trail trees. She wrote,

"A good example of these Indian Trail trees as they are called is the tall hickory at Madison, WIS on the route of an old trail, one whose branches is conspicuously bent into a horizontal position as if to indicate a certain direction. Another Trail tree at County Line, Glencoe, Ill, by the side of the railroad has an odd appearance; perhaps fifteen feet above the ground level, its trunk is bent downward to the earth and then upward again, forming a shape elbow, a few feet above which it forks and then continues up, its leafy branches rising to a good height."[11]

Dr. Raymond E. Janssen, a geologist, also from Evanston, ILL, became interested in the Indian trails and Indian trees and began researching and writing about them in 1934 when he published an article in *American Forests* and then again in 1938 in the *Nature Magazine*.[12] He published a more detail accounting of his finding in the *Scientific Monthly Journal* in 1941 entitled, *Living Guide-Posts of the Past*.[13]

Janssen reported in his observations that,

> *"These trees exhibit an acute or right angle bend in their main trunks, usually from two to five feet above their bases. Rising vertically from the bent trunks are one or more lateral stems, or secondary trunks, bearing the branching structure and leaves. Ages of the trees range from somewhat more than a hundred to two and three hundred years."*[13]

In his first article in *American Forests*[14], he reported that in 1934, there were seventy-five of the trails trees still alive in the Chicago area.

Janssen's report in *Scientific Monthly* covers several years of observation about the trees and he went on to report his conclusions on how the trees were bent and tended over several years. He reported in his observations that he had determined from a personal communication with Dr. Faye-Cooper Cole of the University of Chicago that natives living in the jungles of the Philippine Islands were bending trees using some of the methods he conjectured.

Probably the single most important piece of evidence about the trail trees in the north central part of the country is found in a lawsuit against the Wood County Parks and Forestry, Woods County, Wisconsin. In 1999, Woods County officials filed a plan to cut down 1,500 trees on Skunk Hill located in the Powers Bluff Park to expand a ski slope for recreational use. However, the Potawatomi, Menominee and Ho-Chunk Indian had lived on or near that site up until 1930 and that site was a sacred site. Many of their ancestors were buried there and their graves were marked by trees that were bent by the Indi-

ans. With the aid
of Midwest En-
vironmental Ad-
vocated, a pro-
bono law firm,
the Indians filed
a suit in April
2001 against the
county to stop
destruction   of
the trees and the
sacred burial lo-
cations. Some of
the Indian trees
were cut down

Figure 2-1 Ho-Chunk Trail Tree

before the logging could be stopped. A picture of one of the
Indian trees on Skunk Hill is shown in Figure 2-1.

The Ho-Chunk Nation, called the Winnebago by explorers
entering Wisconsin in the 17th century, were a nomadic tribe
whose territory covered parts of Wisconsin, Minnesota, Illinois, and Iowa. The Ho-Chunk people traveled this four-state
territory on foot and buried their dead along the trails. Traces of villages and campsites where they stayed and worked in
gardens still remain. To help them remember where important
sites were, the Ho-Chunk shaped "marker trees." Marker trees
sometimes indicated gravesites, village sites, or springs. They
also at times pointed out the direction of the trail or a low spot
at which to cross the river.

Since many are being destroyed by storms, or being cut
down by people who do not recognize their significance, the
Indian trees are being documented.[15] Other Native American
cultural resources, like burial sites, are also being documented
and protected. The Ho-Chunk elders, who remember where
many burial sites are, relay the information to the Ho-Chunk
Department of Natural Resources (DNR) office. The DNR
staff then locates the sites and uses ground-penetrating radar
(GPR) to determine, without disturbing the site, if there are

remains under the ground. Once confirmed, these sites are mapped for use by the Ho-Chunk Nation. However, in order to protect sites from possible vandalism, the information is not released to the public.[15]

Another source of information about Indian trees in the Wisconsin area is R. Bruce Allison's book, Every Root and Anchor, Wisconsin's Famous and Historic Trees.[16] Allison's book devotes a whole chapter to Indian trees located in Wisconsin. One Indian tree of note is located on old Highway 81 in Green County. This burr oak tree was known as the Indian Half-Way Tree and marked the halfway distance between Lake Michigan and the Mississippi River. A family that bought the property where the tree is located in1857, told the story of an Indian chief stopping to visit them after they bought the property and cautioning them not to cut the tree down because it was important to the Indians in their travels along the Indian Trail. A marker placed at the tree says,

> "This Burr Oak marks the halfway point between Lake Michigan and the Mississippi River, paced off by Indian runner and confirmed by a US survey of 1832."[16]

Another author, Robert E. Ritzenthaler, in The Wisconsin Archeologist in September 1965, summarized the findings of many people who had located trail trees in many different states. He also commented on how he surmised the trees to have been bent.[17] Mr. Ritzerthaler's summary of tree locations with references included the Chicago area, Mississippi Valley, Texas, Great Smokey Mountains, Pocono Mountains, Southern Illinois, Michigan, Wisconsin, Ohio, Indiana, Kentucky, Tennessee, Missouri, and Arkansas. He also cited a report by Dorothy Moulding Brown in The Wisconsin Archeologist (Vol 19, #2) about other types of Indian trail markings. Ms. Brown wrote,

> "In the city of Milwaukee near the intersection of West Wells and North Thirteen streets, there is reported to have stood in the middle 1830's a large beech

*tree upon the trunk of which there was cut an In-
dian figure with a bow in one hand and an arrow
in the other. The arrow pointed to the south toward
the Menominee River and the bow to the north toward the Milwaukee River. The tree was destroyed
in the improvement of this part of the city. Throughout the period of the 20th Century a number of news
articles where published about Trail trees and Indian Trails."*[17]

Teresa Mattux wrote an article entitled *Timber Talk in Bittersweet,* a Springfield-Green County, Missouri, library publication.[18] She reported finding several bent trees on land near
Springfield, Missouri, that led to a water source. She also
found other bent trees near Buffalo, Missouri, and in Cam-
den County, Missouri. Other articles appeared in *Life Magazine,* July 5, 1963; *Missouri Life,* October 2007; *the Greater St.
Louis Archeological Society* by Dana Elliott, Professor of Biol-
ogy, Central Methodist College, Fayette, Missouri, and others
too numerous to mention.

Articles also appeared in the *Decatur* (Alabama) *Daily News*
in July and August 2006. In the July article, the reporter interviewed Paul Prince, owner of a tract of land in Morgan County Alabama. On that land is an Indian trail tree and an Indian
camping/village site. Paul told the reporter,

*"One local resident lived in an old log cabin across the
creek. He is dead now, but his grandmother said her
great grandmother until she was 12 years old would
stand on the back porch of her log cabin and occa-
sionally see the Indians go through the trail where the
tree is located."*[9]

Some government agencies have also commented on the
Trail trees. USDA Forest Service published a brochure in the
1970's with pictures of some of the Trail Trees found in Missouri on the front cover. The US Fish and Wildlife Service, Region 3 Midwest internet site has a short discussion on the trees
under its *Native Americans – The First People* section.

Video-taped Interviews with Tribal Elders and "Old Timers"

Some tribal elders have been reluctant to talk about the bent trees since their trust of white men has been shattered continuously through several centuries of broken treaties and promises. Others don't know about the trees since their knowledge about the tress was lost with the loss of their culture *(see Chapter 3)*. However, several tribal elders know of their existence and have been willing to share what they know during filmed interviews as part of the development of the documentary *Mystery of the Trees.*

The Lewis & Clark Bicentennial Celebration was held in St. Louis in 2004. As part of the Lewis and Clark Celebration members of the Osage Nation, the first Indians to be encountered by the Lewis and Clark expedition were invited to return to St. Louis to plant a tree to mark and honor the ancient Osage presence in the St. Louis region. The reason for planting the tree was explained by Osage Chief Jim Gray who told the celebration planners about the Osage Indian use of marker trees as guides to special places, paths, or water. Osage Elder Eddy Red Eagle collaborated on the planning for the tree planting ceremony. The ceremony involved planting an Osage orange tree inside a red oak that had been stuck by lightning and burned. Red oak is special to the Osage Indians.

One low growing branch was drawn through a slot cut in the east side of the trunk. This branch was manipulated and tethered in the old way of the Osage so that it formed a marking arm directing the Osage gaze in an easterly direction. The Osage consider that they are always traveling in an easterly direction on their life paths. The Tree-in-Tree is shown in Figure 2-2.

At the Osage Nation In 2008, Eddy Red Eagle was shown many pictures of bent trees that may be attributed to his Osage ancestors. He commented,

> "These trees are tangible evidence of the Osage presence (in Missouri and Arkansas). He said, We don't know how to do this (bend the trees) and even if we did, we can't do this today."[20]

Figure 2-2 Osage Tree in Tree, St. Louis

Celinda Kaelin, past President of the Pike Peak Historical Society and author of *American Indians of the Pikes Peak Region,* annually hosts Ute Indian elders and children as they visit their homelands in the Florissant, Colorado, area. Celinda has been a leader in the discovery of the bent and peeled Indian trees in that part of Colorado. In August 2008, Loya Arum, a Ute elder was interviewed about the Indian trees attributed to the Ute ancestors. Loya said,

"Most of the bent trees point to Pikes Peak, a scared mountain to the Utes."[21]

Loya talked about how members of her tribe would make pilgrimages to Pikes Peak from Crystal Mountain. On the way, they would bend ponderosa pine to the ground. They called these trees prayer trees. The Utes would offer prayers to the trees, their ancestors, themselves and others always approaching the tree from the west as they were told to do.

Loya said,

"When the Ute prayed at a prayer tree they believed their ancestors were present."[21]

The Utes would pray for their ancestor to let them know they cared for them. Loya went on to say that when she was near the Indian trees and trails that she would think,

"Wow! I'm walking on the trail where my ancestors walked."[21]

Loya confirmed that the bent, prayer and peeled trees on the high Colorado plains were the work of the Utes.

Billy Shaw is of Cherokee descent. Billy, along with Lamar Marshall, was interviewed sitting by a trail tree located on the Benge Trail of Tears route southeast of Huntsville, Alabama, in 2007. Billy said about the bent trees that,

"they marked trails, and marked different things like water, shelter and direction. I'm thinking they also marked ceremonial places."[22]

The bent tree on the mountain portion of the Benge Route was bent long before the trail was used during the removal of the Cherokees.

A number of Comanche elders were interviewed about the bent Comanche tree found in Dallas, Texas by Linda Pelon. This pecan tree, that was found to be 290 years old in 1997 when it died, was believed to have marked a Comanche camp site and the *Story telling place.*[23] The Comanches were a nomadic tribe that traveled the western plains to places able to sustain their peoples' life style. These places were usually along a river or stream and were flat enough so that their teepees could be put on the level ground. Many of these camp sites were marked by the Comanche with a tree that had been bent low to the ground sometimes in a rainbow shape. The Comanche camp site mentioned above is located in Gateway Park in Dallas, Texas. In 1997, the Comanche Nation proclaimed the Gateway Park marker tree as a living monument to our historic presence.[23]

Near the location of the bent pecan tree is another Comanche site in a Trinity Forest park location. This site is located on a bluff above the river and camp site and had a natural amphitheater appearance. The Comanches who visited this site in 2002, believe it was used for storytelling. The Comanche stories were passed on orally from generation to generation. These stories perpetuated the Comanche customs and history. They were very important in teaching the children.[23]

Tom Belt, a Western Nation Cherokee, in his interview said,

> *"These roads, these paths, these byways were places where people have traveled were much, much more important and much older than anybody could imagine. The way in which they marked them, the bending of trees, rocks, rock cairns where essentially very old markers. The marking of these places along the way were not just markers of the trail but markers for specific places or pointing to specific areas. These markers and these roads were not just markers from one side of the mountain to the other. But they were part of a great highway system that allowed people from many tribes to interact with each other."*

Old Timer Interviews

Because of the loss of culture *(see Chapter 3)*, many tribal elders no longer know the history of Trail tree use in the Indian way of life. However, some of the knowledge about the trees has been passed down through stories by the *old timers* who either encoun- tered an Indian who told them or learned about them from grand- parents or great- grandparents.

With each in- terview, more understanding about the Indian

Figure 2-3 Florissant, Colorado Trail Tree

trees was learned helping to piece together this lost cultural aspect of the Indian way of life. Several of the significant interviews are included in this chapter.

Toby Wells was raised on a potato farm in the Florissant, Colorado area in the mid-1900s. One day, when he was about ten years old, a Ute Indian lady approached their farm when his parents were away. The Indian asked Toby if he knew of a spring and an oddly shaped tree nearby. Toby took the Ute Indian to see the spring and oddly shaped tree near their farm house. Toby told her,

"We get our drinking water from this spring and I play on the tree you are mentioning everyday."[24]

The Indian told Toby that there was a Ute trail that went by the bent tree and that the tree marked the site of the spring and a chipping site. The unusual shaped tree is shown in Figure 2-3. The Ute trail can still be seen passing by the tree.

Shawn Frizzel, a Ranger at the Florissant Fossil Bed National Monument in Colorado, was interviewed about the Indian trees on the monument property. She said,

"We have twenty-seven of the bent trees and a number of the peeled trees at the park which are being preserved. As we take people onto the park, we tell them about what we have learned about these trees from the descendents of the first people on this land."[25]

Throughout the home lands of the Ute Indians in the Florissant area are many bent trees. They were found along roads and old trails. Eleven Mile State Park and Mueller State Park also have bent trees. One of the trees, a ponderosa pine, from Mueller State Park is shown in Figure 2-4.

James Lewis bought a large farm in central Arkansas. On that farm was an oddly shaped tree that looked like a large *four*. In his interview, James said he "bought the farm property in 1978, and the tree was there then. My neighbor told me about the tree." He said,

"The old timers said it was an Indian tree. The Indian trees in that area either pointed to hang over bluffs or to springs. This tree points to Tomahawk Spring which is located over the hill from the tree."[26]

The tree is shown in Figure 2-5. South of Birmingham, Alabama, there is an almost identical tree which points to a stream.

Lamar Marshall, Cultural Heritage Director, WildSouth, Inc., has spent the last 20 years researching and writing about Indian culture in the southeast associated with the Cherokees,

Figure 2-4 Mueller State Park, Colorado Tree

Creeks, Choctaw and Chickasaw Indians. He is one of the most knowledgeable persons on Indian culture other than tribal elders. He was interview in the Buckhead National Forest in Alabama, at the site of one of the major Indian battles. The tree in Figure 2-6 is at that location. Lamar said,

"They are scattered all over the forest here. There is some type of pattern to the trees. If you were to lay out and grid out the Native American trails, these trees would coincide with the trails. There is no doubt about that in my experience."[27]

Books on Indian Trees, Trails and Other Writings

One of the earliest accounts written that provided insight into the Indian trails is the journal account of Lucius Verus Bierce published as book entitled, *Travels in the Southlands, 1822-1823.*[28]

Lucius Bierce, having graduated from an Ohio University in October 1822, set out to walk/ride along the Indian trails and early settler roads of a young growing nation. He wrote a journal account of his travels that allows researchers to determine his whereabouts fairly accurately. His travels took him southeast to South Carolina where he joined with a group in four wagons in 1823, and began his adventure through the Cherokee territory in Georgia, Alabama, and Tennessee fifteen years before the Cherokees were removed from this part of the nation. His journey account provides extensive details of the trails he traveled and the Cherokees he met along the way. His trip took about one year's time and he returned to Ohio late in 1823.

Figure 2-5 Arkansas Tree

Other accounts of the Indian trails and Indian villages can be found in the writings of Benjamin Hawkins[29], Indian agent to the Creeks and Cherokees; John Gerar William De Brahm[30], Surveyor General to the King of England; William Bartram[31], naturalist; John Goff[32] and many more.

Although these early explorers traveled the trails, sometimes guided and sometimes not, they had to know how to

Figure 2-6 Bankhead National Forest Tree

follow the extensive trail systems of their time without getting lost. Surely, they must have known about the trails markers but unfortunately none of them commented on them.

George Featherstonhaugh, the first Geologist of the United States and surveyor of the Louisiana Purchase, also wrote journal accounts of his traveling the Indian trails and published them in the *Monthly American Journal of Geology and Natural History*. Some of his journal accounts are contained in letters he wrote which are now housed in the Missouri Historical Archives. The collection consists of thirteen letters—eleven written by G.W. Featherstonhaugh to Colonel John J. Abert and two written by Thomas Fitzpatrick to Lieutenant James W. Abert. The Featherstonhaugh letters were written from various locales including Detroit, Green Bay, Prairie du Chien, North Carolina, and Quebec. He related details about his explorations, including geological reports, descriptions of flora, fauna, and the people encountered, and difficulties with terrain and conditions. In a journal account dated August 25, 1837, George wrote,

> *"Our way led through a succession of vales separated from each other by mountains of highly micaceous gneiss about eight hundred feet high, with innumerable streamlets flowing through them. The county was perfectly wild, without any roads but obscure Indian trails almost hidden by the scrubs and high grass."*[33]

Two books that draw the most attention regarding the existence of Indian trail trees are *Cry of the Eagle* by Forest Wade[34] and *Indian Trail Trees* by Elaine Jordan.[35]

Forest Wade, part Cherokee, lived in Forsyth County, Georgia, where Cherokee Chief Rising Fawn and his Red Bank tribe existed until removed on the Trail of Tears in 1838. Two other Cherokee tribes lived near the Red Bank Cherokees. They were the Long Swamp Cherokees and the Big Savannah Cherokees, but both of these settlements had ceased to exist long before the Trail of Tears removal.

Forest Wade spent time with his father and later was taught by other Cherokees how to read the symbols left by the Cherokees to mark sites in the forests where the Indians had lived. Some of these symbols were bent Indian trees and others consisted of symbols carved on the skin of beech trees. Wade's book has many pictures of the trail trees he discovered in north Georgia. He even drew sketches of some types of Indian trees naming their particular shapes.

Forest Wade spent 25 years following hundreds of Indian trails and deciphering their symbols, carefully recording them for future reference. He said,

"This knowledge, forbidden to the white race, was so secret that death was the penalty to any Cherokee who revealed it to anyone other than their own race or blood brother."[34]

Forest Wade's daughter, Peggy Dorsey, told the authors that Western Nation Cherokees often visited her father to learn how to read the signs and perhaps to recover some of the gold buried along the Etowah River by their ancestors before they were removed to Oklahoma.

Elaine Jordan moved to Ellijay, Georgia, in 1988 to continue her writing career. While living in this north Georgia community she became exposed to the mysterious Indian trail trees that exited in the area. The subject of the trail trees intrigued her so she began extensive research on the subject and, with the help of her children and friends, she began searching several north Georgia counties to see if she could locate a few of these mysterious trees. She found over 300 trees which are documented in her book which was published in 1997.

Elaine's book was the first book on Indian trees to get a wider national distribution. That led to many of the follow-on efforts to expand the understanding of the trail trees including the work of the Trail Tree Project. Through Elaine's mentoring, the Trail Tree Project team has continued to research the subject extensively, and this book is the results of that research.

Unfortunately, the locations of many of the trees discovered by Elaine were not documented exactly, so they are lost again. Over time they will be rediscovered as more folks trek through the forests looking for them. However, they will have to be found without Elaine's help as she passed away in 2009.

One last book to mention, *Indian Trails of the Warrior Mountains*,[36] was written by Rickey Butch Walker and Lamar Marshall. Ricky Butch Walker, a descendant of Creek and Cherokee heritage, spent a lifetime in the forest following old Indian paths and trails and being taught by his grandparents. Before his retirement, he conveying that knowledge to the school children in the Lawrence County, Alabama, Indian Studies Program and to the general public through his book. No greater collection of information on Indian trails and related Indian sites exists for a southern state.

Lamar Marshall, WildSouth Cultural Heritage Officer, is one of the foremost researchers on Indian trails and Indian sites. In 2009, he and Gail King completed a study which located and documented the Benge Trail of Tears route through Alabama. This study has set a precedent for all other studies of this type to follow.

Laura Hubler was not a writer of books on Indian trees or trails. Rather, she was a prolific writer of letters, reports and other documentation on the Indian trees she located in the Mark Twain National Forest in Missouri. Her writings are contained in multiple boxes placed in an archive in Arkansas.

Beginning in the late 1960s and continuing on to the 1980s, she single-handily encouraged and sometimes pushed Forest Service Rangers, cohorts, friends, neighbors, and others to help her in her quest to find Indian trees in Missouri, Arkansas, Kansas and other states. Her quest to locate and preserve these trees began, "When an Indian friend informed her that the Forest Service, in its ignorance, had decided to destroy all of what was termed the useless deformed trees."[37] In response to her dedicated work, Laura was presented with three white feathers to signify her new name, Three Feathers, by a Choctaw Indian friend.

"The Choctaw Indian explained that the feathers were not given; they were earned by deeds of great significance to the Indians. It was her efforts toward educating the public and saving the legacy that earned her the feather award and her Indian name."[38] He further said,

"It is rare for a squaw to wear more than one feather. What she has done is not for one tribe, but for every tribe in the timbered country."[38]

Her archived materials contain hundreds of pictures of bent trees throughout the Midwest and elsewhere. Unfortunately, like Elaine Jordan, she did not have the use of GPS technology, so she was unable to accurately document the location of the trees she found on maps with the exception of a few locations. Where she did record the location on simple maps, those trees have been located forty years after she had found them.

Laura spent a lot of time befriending a Blackfoot Indian she called Hannibal Pete. Although not his real name, Hannibal Pete did begin to share some of the information about the Indian trees with Laura. In one poorly recorded audio taped interview with him, he told her that she had discovered some of the secrets about the trees. He took her to several locations and explained some of the meaning of the trees to her but little remains of these disclosures.

The Overwhelming Evidence in the Number of Trees Still Living

In March 2007, when the National Trail Tree Project was started, there were just over 100 trees in the Mountain Stewards database. All of these located and documented trees were from a few counties in north Georgia. The Trail Tree Project team that met in Hobbs State Park, Arkansas, had many more trees in their personal database and agreed to add them to the national database. Throughout the remainder of 2007, the number of trees in the database grew rapidly passing 614 trees by September 2007 encompassing four states and passed the 700 mark by the end of December 2007.

The Mountain Stewards added a Trail Tree Project section to its website in late 2007. It became obvious that the subject of Trail Trees was of great interest to many across the country since the hits on the web site began to grow exponentially. The number of people viewing the website resulted in many inquiries for more data information. The website was expanded to allow people interesting in the Trail Tree Project to submit trees they had located. That resulted in many more people getting involved with the project and some becoming fulltime team members in researching trail trees.

With the expanded number of people searching the country for trail trees, the database had grown to 1,067 trees near the end of 2008. Trees had been found in twenty-eight states by then.

In 2009, the number of hits on the web site regarding trail trees grew to over 9,000 each month. The growth continued as more people become aware of this aspect of Indian culture.

The technology of the internet coupled with its built-in search engines has increased communication beyond the imaginable. With the click of your mouse and few search terms, everything you want to know on a subject appears on your screen instantaneously. This ever-expanding capability has made it possible for a few people working on the discovery of a lost Indian culture to reach out to thousands who are interested in joining them in the search. At the end of 2010, the number of trees located and documented has grown to over 1,600 covering thirty-nine states and Canada as shown in the Figure 2-7. In 2011, the number is now 1,750 trees. The states shown in green indicate where trail trees have been located physically or where a report documenting their existence has been found. States shown in orange are the *peeled trees* or culturally modified trees which have been found related to the western Indian tribes. The culturally modified trees are also reported to have existed in the northeastern United States but none of the trees have been reported by early 2010. The trail trees may well exist in the rest of states not highlighted, but they have not been yet reported.

The evidence of finding trail trees in thirty-nine states, many of which are similar in shape, as well as the total number located so far can not be discounted or attributed to nature. The statistics of the numbers and similarities overwhelming show these trees are not bent by natural occurrences but rather by human intervention.

Figure 2-7 States with Trees Located Through 2010

It is particularly interesting to follow the migration of the Cherokees and the existence of similar bent trees where they lived.

After the Revolutionary War, the Cherokees who sided with the British were punished by the US government. Prior to the war as shown in Figure 2-8, the Cherokees claimed territory covering parts of the Carolinas, Virginia, West Virginia, north Georgian and Alabama, and most of Tennessee and Kentucky.

The Cherokees were forced to cede over half of their claimed territory after the war because they fought with the British. The colonists, who had been held back from migrating into Indian Territory, now wanted freedom to move into these frontier areas. Many Cherokees saw this expansion as a time to move further west to a place where the white man wound not interfere with their way of life.

One of the first migrations westward of the Cherokees began in the late 1700s. The Cherokees contacted the Spanish Governor in 1788 and gained permission to settle west of the Mississippi. A group of Cherokees moved there in 1790. It is not known how many Cherokee settlements moved west at this time, but it is known that Cherokee and Shawnee were frequent visitors to the area controlled by the Spanish. These Cherokees settled in the area of the St. Francis River in what is now Arkansas. Another group of Cherokees from the Chickamauga settlements moved west in 1794 and still other Cherokees moved there in 1807-1808.

After the Louisiana Purchase was made by the United States, President Thomas Jefferson began encouraging the Congress to begin efforts to remove all Indians east of the Mississippi. In 1808, the Secretary of War instructed their agent, Colonel Meigs, to use every inducement to get the Cherokees to exchange their land for land west of the Mississippi. The government offered an area of land between the Arkansas and White Rivers (present northern Arkansas) sufficient to support their hunting life. A delegation of Cherokees visited in 1809. The reports of this land were favorable and a large number of Cherokees in the area agreed to move.

In 1810, Duwali (or The Bowl), Tsulawi (or Fox), and Talontuskee moved their villages west of the Mississippi. Duwali, a half-blood, was chief of his town of Little Hiwassee (present western North Carolina). Talontuskee became the nominal leader of all the western Cherokees. These and other groups moving west settled on the White and St Francis Rivers in present northeast Arkansas while others settled on either side of the Arkansas River in present west-central Arkansas.

Because so many Cherokees had moved into the Arkansas territory which had been part of the Osage homeland, numerous conflicts occurred including some fierce battles between several of the tribes in the area. Finally, the eastern Cherokees, against their wishes, had to cede more lands to allow the western Cherokees to gain ownership of hunting lands in Arkansas which occurred at the signing of the Turkeytown Treaty in 1817. That treaty took land away from the Osage and gave to the Cherokees land between the Arkansas and White rivers. More Cherokees moved west

Figure 2-8 Cherokee Territory Claims - 1770

based on these further cessions of Cherokee eastern land.

Figure 2-9 shows the boundaries of the Cherokee Territory in Arkansas in 1817. Each yellow square on the map indicates the location of a located trail tree, many of which are inside the boundaries of their new territory.

Figure 2-9 Trail Trees in Arkansas

However, prior to 1817, the Cherokees were not confined to these boundaries but co-existed with the Osage and Shawnees who lived in the Arkansas Territory prior to it becoming a state in 1836.

The hundreds of trail trees found in Arkansas could easily be considered as being from almost any other state as their shapes are so similar they can not be distinguished from each other as seen in Figures 2-10, 2-11, 2-12 and 2-13.

Figure 2-10 Arkansas Tree

Figure 2-11 Georgia Tree

Trees with a Documented History

Many of the Indian trees that have been found are from a period covering the last three decades. But there are few trees that have a documented history of their existence that is longer than 30 years. These trees are clearly demonstrating the fact that the bent trees are stunted in their growth and little change in the tree can be ob-

Figure 2-12 Alabama Tree

served over a fifty to seventy year period.

Henry Rowe Schoolcraft explored the United States in the early 1800s and documented his findings in his book.[52] In the 1818-

Figure 2-13 Arkansas Tree

1819 period, he explored the Missouri territory and wrote a journal account, *Journal of 1818–1819 Tour of the Ozarks*, published by Missouri State University. Schoolcraft documented in his journal the existence of one of the largest caves in Missouri known as Smallin Cave. Smallin Cave located in Christian County, Missouri, was home to Osage Indians, and it is likely that members of the Cherokee tribe also lived here. Near the cave entrance is an Indian trail tree. In 1941, Harriett Mills as a young girl visited the cave and had her picture taken sitting on the trail tree as shown in Figure 2-14. She visited the cave again in 2009, 68 years later and had her picture taken again sitting on the same tree as seen in Figure 2-15. Comparing the two pictures, we see that the tree has not grown in size significantly in sixty-eight years.

Figure 2-14 Harriet Mills on Smallin Cave Tree - 1941

Laura Hubler did extensive research on the Indian trees in Missouri in the period from 1960 to 1980. In the early 1960s she documented a number of Indian trees located in then Clark National Forest (now Mark Twain National Forest) west of Ironton, Missouri. She named the trees and published a report on a number of them. One of them she called the *Old Horse-Head* which points down a hill to a water source. That tree was rediscovered in 2009, based on directions written by

Figure 2-15 Harriet Mills on Smallin Cave Tree - 2009

Figure 2-16 Laura Hubler's "Old Horse-Head" Tree

Laura about forty-five years previously. The tree is shown in Figure 2-16 and looks very much like it did in her drawings of the tree from the 1960s.

Chapter 4 will provide a more detailed analysis of the many trail trees located throughout the United States and discuss their similarities in more depth.

Also, in Chapter 5, the very different bent or modified trees of the Comanche, Ute and other western tribes will be discussed.

Chapter 3

MYSTERY OF THE TREES – A LOSS OF INDIAN CULTURE

The question that begs to be answered is why is there so little written or spoken information about the trees bent by the Native Americans. Answering that question requires study about history and Indian culture.

It is important to understand how information was passed along to the next generation. Rather than going to school and studying textbooks detailing their culture, the Indians were an oral society. There was little written down about their stories, their myths, and their ways of doing things. The elders were the keepers of the stories and the tribal history. Whether meeting one-on-one or at a gathering of the entire clan, the elders told their stories and taught the Indian way of life to those younger than they. In the telling of the stories, the continuity of tribal culture was preserved. Lose the elders and you lose not only the past but also the future of the tribe.

In order to understand how the elders were lost, how most aspects of the native culture changed, and why the story of the trees is difficult to find, it is necessary to go all the way back to 1492, when Christopher Columbus arrived in San Salvador. From that point on, life for those who already lived in the New World began to change. In less than 400 years, native population numbers were decimated! From the Canadian Arctic to South America, native people were subjected to previously unknown diseases, torture, murder, forced labor, starvation, warfare, forced relocations, destruction of their food supplies, and actions by governments and religious organizations that set out to destroy, and were successful in destroying, native culture and religious heritage.

There is no way to know for certain the number of indigenous people who lived in what are now Canada and the continental United States when Columbus arrived. Estimates range from as low as 1.8 million to as many as 112 million people. Since there are no hard data from that time, reliable statistics are difficult, or impossible, to produce. After much research, Russell Thornton estimated that there were 72+ million American Indians in the Western Hemisphere in 1492. Five million lived in what is now the United States. By 1800 that five million had declined to 600,000 and by the last decade of the nineteenth century the number had dropped to 250,000![39] The elders, the storytellers, the keepers of the history were a part of those who were lost. As David Stannard said,

"Within no more than a handful of generations following their first contact with Europeans, the vast majority of the western hemisphere's native peoples had been exterminated."[40]

DISEASE

While scholars agree that after contact with Europeans the number of native peoples plummeted, the extent and causes of that decline have long been debated. However, nearly all agree that the introduction of epidemic diseases, to which the natives had no immunity, was the major cause for the decline. The scope of the epidemics over the years was almost unbelievable. It is possible that in some areas more than 90% of the population perished. In comparison, 33% of those exposed to the Black Death in medieval Europe were killed.[41]

One of the most devastating diseases was smallpox, but typhus, measles, influenza, bubonic plague, cholera, malaria, tuberculosis, mumps, yellow fever, and whooping cough also came along with the Europeans. Since the native people were subjected to several previously unknown diseases at once, the toll was even more devastating.

OTHER CAUSES FOR DECLINING POPULATION

Certainly, diseases were the leading cause of the population decline, but there were other factors as well, all of which were related to the coming of the European explorers and settlers. One factor was warfare. Again lack of written record makes it difficult to say just what warfare was like before the arrival of Columbus. However, there is no debate about the fact that warfare became deadlier after the arrival of the Europeans. Firearms, gunpowder, and swords, all made killing easier. The role of the horse was also important. Can you imagine the reaction of a native person, fighting on foot with a bow and arrows, and a stone headed club, as powerfully armed strangers bore down on him from the backs of these huge never-before-seen beasts?

Attitudes towards warfare worked against the native peoples as well. War for the Indians often had some ritualistic component, or was fueled by a desire to right a wrong. Once there had been retaliation for the wrong, the war ended. Some tribes such as the Cherokees met together at a *ball game*, a very fierce and violent game that took the place of what we would call a traditional war. Europeans, on the other hand, fought for total unconditional victory.

When the European fought, they had resources to sustain the conflict over several years. Native people seldom had stored resources that would last for more than a few months. Making matters worse for the Indians, Europeans often caused starvation and further death by destroying, usually by burning, what crops and stored goods the natives might have had.

As the years passed, more Europeans came to colonize the land. With each influx of settlers, more land was needed. Starting from the east coast of America, the Indians were constantly pushed into lands not yet wanted by the whites. Sometimes the land was acquired by treaty. On rare occasions, the settlers, and even some governments, engaged in what is called *democides*. Tribes who were seen as a hindrance to expansions were simply killed.[42] From the beginning, the prevailing attitude toward the Native Americans was negative. Since most Europeans saw them as savages, devil worshippers, uneducated, beyond the salvation of the church, and not to be trusted, exterminating them became acceptable.[43]

In the early eighteenth century the states of Massachusetts, Connecticut and New Jersey imposed a *scalp bounty* on dead Indians. By 1723 the price had soared to 100 pounds for a scalp. Ward Churchill wrote:

'Indeed, in many areas it (murdering Indians) quickly became an outright business.'[44]

George Washington called them *beast of prey* and called for their total destruction.[45] Later, Thomas Jefferson was one of the first to advocate that they be removed to the west – far beyond where English settlements were expected to spring up.

In 1848, before the gold rush in California, the native population was estimated to have been 150,000. In 1870, after the gold rush, the number had dropped to 31,000. Again, much of the decline can be attributed to diseases brought in by the hundreds of thousands of gold seekers. However, in 1851, extermination of all the surviving natives was urged by the Governor of California.[46] In fact, after 1849, in California, an Indian scalp brought the magnificent sum of 25 cents! Articles in the Rocky Mountain News from Denver and the Santa Fe New Mexican agreed with the Governor of California's extermination policy.[47]

We have certainly begun to answer the question: "What happened to the elders, the storytellers, the keepers of the history?" Disease, warfare, exploitation, massacres all played their part in their loss.

CULTURE

Indian culture was very different from colonial culture. The colonists did not understand the Indian concept of shared ownership of the land, respect for all living things or, what we would call today, environmental conservation. Living lightly on the land, using only what you needed, was completely foreign to those who came to America to settle. They wanted to own their own land, have nicer and fancier accouterments of life, increase their personal wealth and, in every way, *better* themselves.

The Indian way of life was built on hunting and gathering to support their food and medicinal needs. They did a little farming to augment their daily dietary requirements. It was basically a subsistence society. The bow and arrow allowed a man to gather in enough meat to feed his family and to help with feeding others in the tribe. Simple utensils, of stone, bone, or pottery, and baskets made from reeds allowed the women to farm, make clothes and keep the family supplied with their everyday needs. They did not have metal utensils or weapons.

After the earliest contact with the Spanish, French and English, traders came along, bringing with them guns, swords, metal knives, sewing utensils, woven cloth, pots and pans, and farming implements. The Indians quickly saw the advantage in having these items. Indian culture began to change. Soon they were killing more animals then they needed for survival in order to have hides to trade with the white man. In South Carolina alone in the mid 1700s, over a million hides were brought to the port of Charleston by the Indians.[30] The same thing was taking place in Georgia as reported by the King's Chief Surveyor, John Gerar William De Brahm.[30] The Indians put away their bows and arrows and picked up the long rifle and metal knives. The woman began learning to sew with fine needles. They began to make clothing from cloth provided by the traders and the traditional buckskin was replaced. Somewhat nomadic tribes began to settle in one place to farm and raise livestock.

The Indians rapidly became dependent on the white man's goods. As interaction increased between the two divergent cultures, many Indians began to adopt, more and more, the white man's culture. The reasons for doing things the old ways changed and the old ways began to disappear. Indian culture would never be the same.

Missionaries also played a role in altering the culture of the Indians. Catholic missionaries in what is now California were the first to come. It was over a century after the first missions were established in California before the first Protestant mission was founded in Massachusetts. In general, the Catholic missionaries sought simple expressions of faith from the Indians. Protestant missionaries, on the other hand, sought not only to convert the Indians to Christianity but also to convert them to a European lifestyle. Many of these men believed that it was their God-given duty to bring the *savages* to Christ. Being a Christian was of supreme importance, but *being a Christian* also required living life as it was known by the Europeans. The original way of life of the Indians could no longer be allowed to exist. Many cultural changes had already taken place, but the Protestant missionaries were the first to intentionally begin to try to transform the *savage* culture to one that was *civilized and proper.*

The Indians way of life, their mythical tribal stories, their belief systems, their languages, and their customs must be changed. In an effort to counteract the influence of the native culture, schools and mission sites were developed. The missionaries encouraged the Indians to bring their children to the mission to be taught not only to read and write but also how to live the European way of life.

One branch of the Cherokee even changed the format of their government to match that of the white man. They hoped that if they changed their ways, they would be able to remain in what was left of their homelands and co-exist in peace with the settlers. This proved not to be true.

Some Indians considered this unwanted influence on their lives very harmful. They advocated separation from the white man and a return to their traditional way of life. With each new step of change, with each new push by white settlers for more land, they saw more of their culture forgotten. Some of these Indians settled in the nearly inaccessible mountains of what is now North Carolina. Others began to move farther west as early as 1790.

For those who continued to have contact with the white man, their stories about how to live freely in the forest were no longer being taught by the elders. The reasons for particular activities were disappearing. Perhaps this is part of the reason why the mystery of the bent trees is with us today. With the influx of people, the trails, the sites for finding water, shelter, or medicinal plants no longer needed to be marked. The seldom-used paths became trading paths, settler's highways, and military transportation routes. Wayside inns sprang up to provide shelter and food. Native medicines were often replaced by those of the white men. There was no need to use the bent trees as signposts.

GEOGRAPHIC RELOCATION

As we have pointed out, from the time of the first explorers and colonists, Native peoples whose homelands blocked the way of colonial expansion were either removed or in some cases destroyed. The government, starting as far back as Thomas Jefferson, began systematically forcing the Indians off their land. Every geographical move resulted in a move away from the life they had known. Promising many things, every treaty written by the government was broken almost before the ink was dry.

In a few places, groups of Indians were allowed to continue living in the area of their homeland on small reservations. After the Revolutionary War, many in the northeast fled to Canada. Today, there are still small reservations that are scattered around the United States but the majority of native peoples have been relocated to Oklahoma.

One of the saddest tales of relocation took place in the mid 1800s. The discovery of gold in Georgia brought the issue of where the Indians could live to a head. The government decided that all Indians had to be removed. Rounded up with little advance warning, they were herded into stockades and finally forced to move west in the cold of winter. This is the one part of the story about which almost everyone has heard. Without much thought, we say, "Oh, yes, the Trail of Tears." And we see in our minds a much-sanitized picture of colorful Indians walking or riding horses as they move west to a new life.

There are very good reasons why the Indians call it the "Trail Where They Cried." It is an example of man's inhumanity to man. In the documentary that has been made about this forced relocation, the Cherokee who suffered the fate of that deadly trip said when they reached Oklahoma,

"We arrived with no future and no past."

They were referring to the fact that they had lost not only the older generation but the younger generation as well on the trail where at least 4,000 are said to have died. The complete story is too much to include in this writing. But when you research the true story of the Indian removal, you will find it heartbreaking.

Some Indians found ways to avoid going on that journey. Ricky Butch Walker, from Alabama, said,

> *"After the Removal Act of 1830, you had to deny your Indian blood if you didn't want to be removed to Oklahoma. So it was a forced choice that my family was under. My grandfather wanted us to know we were of Indian blood, and he told us stories about it, but he would never go out and advocate he was an Indian person."*[48]

Mr. Walker said that those who stayed behind claimed to be Black Dutch or some other nationality so that they would not have to leave their homes.

In an interview with Gail King, also from Alabama, Gail said,

> *"My grandmother buried the family Bible... my grandmother, who was part Indian, did not want to have nothing to do with her Indian heritage. She did everything she could to deny that heritage. She was afraid that her family would be removed to OK."*[49]

A group of the Eastern Cherokee was allowed to remain in North Carolina. And in northwestern South Carolina many natives took to the safety of the rugged mountains and were never found. Having avoided census takers for years, they are just now beginning to reclaim their identity as the Cherokee Bear Clan.

Not only were the Cherokee relocated from Georgia, other tribes were also pushed from their homelands. The Osage, who at one time controlled all of the land from the Mississippi River to the Great Plains, had been pushed into parts of Missouri and Kansas. Next, they were moved out of Missouri and given a long narrow strip of land in Kansas. Then they were driven from that bit of land because those building railroads wanted it. In 1872, they were relocated to their reservation in northeast Oklahoma. Their journey was similar to that of the Cherokee who suffered the Trail of Tears. Eddy Red Eagle, an Osage elder, said that as a youngster, he asked an elder about what life had been like before the tribe was moved to Oklahoma. He went on to say,

> *"In 1700s there were 20,000 Osage. In 1872, only 2000 Osages walked into this river basin reservation alive. It must have hurt so badly that they said they would not talk about it [previous life] no more. And, they didn't. They even made it taboo to talk about it. [The elder told him] The things they did back then - you're not able to think like they did! They made us almost scared to talk about their early life."*[20]

After the tribes had been settled onto the reservations, the government's next step in *civilizing* the Indians was to remove the children. Over 100,000 children were taken from their parents and placed in Indian schools beginning in November 1878, where they were forced to wear the white man's clothing, speak the white man's language, and learn the white man's ways. They were taught, sometimes with painful punishments, that anything *Indian* was inferior and to be strictly avoided. When the children were returned to the reservations, they had been so changed by their experiences they no long fit into their own culture.

In an interview with Barbara Goodin, a Comanche who is an integral part of the effort to re-invigorate the Comanche language, we learned that the harsh experience of having their language and culture literally *beat out of them* resulted in many of them not teaching the Indian way of life to their children. She said,

> *"My husband was raised as a child on the Comanche Reservation. He was not aware of his Comanche heritage back then. His mother was sent to the Ft. Sill Indian School. They literally beat the language out of the children. She still spoke the language in her later years but she never shared their heritage with her children… for fear they would go through what she experienced in the school."*[50]

Like the Comanche, many of the tribes are now working diligently to regain their languages. For some of them, the number of people who can speak the language is very small. In an interview with Kerry Holton, Chief of the Delaware Nation, he said,

> *"If you can't speak the language, you can't sing the songs, you can't tell the stories and you're not an Indian."*[1]

Eddy Red Eagle would agree with him. He said that the Osage language doesn't translate easily into English. Subtle meanings are changed or lost completely.

In summary, due to the dramatic loss of such a large number of people and the changes that rapidly occurred in the native cultures, their languages, stories, songs, and the role trees played in their lives were almost lost as well.

There are those who have stated that their ancestors used trees for many reasons. Treaties were often signed under a particular tree. Trees were used to mark trails or a special place, a place where water, or shelter, or medicinal plants could be found. They were also used to indicate sacred places, graves, and river crossings. The Native Americans themselves did not write about the trees. In fact, according to Forest Wade, a part Cherokee, in his book *Cry of the Eagle*, telling a non-Indian about the trees could result in death.[34] Over the years, however, others have written articles, books, and newspaper accounts about the trees. Based on conversations with native elders from several tribes, and these accounts, it is our belief that these living artifacts do exist and should be preserved.

Chapter 4

INDIAN BENT TREES – TRAIL, MARKER, THONG, SIGNAL, AND MORE

The knowledge of how trees were bent by the Native Americans and for what purpose is lost for now. No elders have been found who know or if they do know, they have been unwilling to talk about the subject. Furthermore, no reference document or tribal historical papers have been located that provides this missing knowledge. Eddy Red Eagle of the Osage Nation commented in his interview, "Even if we knew how they did this, we can not do it today."[20]

This knowledge had to have been handed down orally from elders to the next generation. With the loss of culture reported in Chapter 3, this knowledge slowly disappeared over time. The removal of the Indians from their homelands to Oklahoma was, in all probability, the final coup de grace for this cultural aspect of the Indian way of life. With this loss of knowledge, we can only speculate on how the bending of trees was accomplished.

TREE SPECIES USED BY THE INDIANS

Bending a tree to mark a trail, a water source, graves or other things meant carefully choosing if you wanted it to last long enough to be useful. Thus, the Indians chose species of trees that had long longevity. How they knew which trees had longevity in the hundreds of years is beyond our understanding but they certainly knew. The bent trees that are found today are species that have a life span of 300 years or more. The primarily species of trees used by the Indians are shown in Table 1.

Principal Indian Trail Tree Longevity Table

Common Name	Scientific Name	Longevity (yrs)	Remarks
American Beech	Fagus grandifolia	300-400	Occasional use
Bald Cypress	Taxodium distichum	600+	Occasional use
American Elm	Ulmus armericana	200-300	Mostly in northern US in the 1700's
Hickory's	various	200-300	
Red Maple	Acer rubrum	150-300	Northern US
Sugar Maple	Acer saccharum	300-400	Northern US
Chestnut Oak	Querus prinus	300-400	Occasionally used
White Oak	Quercus alba	300-600	Primary tree used
Red Oak	Quercus rubra	300+	Secondary to White Oak
Burr Oak	Quercus macrocarpa	300+	Mostly in northern US but also in TX
Live Oak	Quercus virginiana	300+	Mostly in southern US
Sweetgum	Liquidambar styracifua	200-300	
Yellow Poplar	Liriodendron tulipifera	250-400	
Pecan	Carya illinoensis	300+	Comanche tree
Sycamore	Platanus occidentalis	300+	
Loblolly Pine	Pinus taeda	200-300	Southern tree
Long Leaf Pine	Pinus paluatris	400-500	Southern tree
Ponderosa Pine	Pinus ponderosa	400+	Western tree

Table 1 – Principal Indian Trail Tree Species

The most commonly found trees in the eastern United States are white oaks followed by red oaks. Also found often are sweetgum and poplars. In the deep-south, a number of bent live oak and pines can also be found. Initially, pines were excluded from consideration as they were considered to be too brittle to have been bent without breaking. However, after finding a large number of them that had the exact same shape, they were added to the Trail Tree database.

In the west, the ponderosa pine was the principal tree used. Pecan and cottonwood trees are often found associated with the marking of Comanche camp sites.

SPECULATION ON HOW THE TREES WERE BENT

Since there appears to be no one remaining who knows how the trees were bent, we are left to speculate on how it was done. However, we are not without some scientific or long-term horticultural experimentation that can help us make an educated theoretical hypothesis.

The knowledge of bending trees was not limited to Native American Indians. In fact, references to tree bending can be found in other cultures.[13] Knowledge about bending trees goes back as far as 200 AD and perhaps further. The Chinese developed the horticulture art form and methodology of bending trees known as Bonsai. Over centuries of time, this art form was perfected into what it has become today and it has now spread to many countries including Japan which has added to the horticultural art form.

With simple tools, tree trunks and branches can be manipulated into many deformations to create oddly shaped trees. With experience, the horticulturists learned how to bend a limb without breaking it and forced it into a particular shape. Some were cut to relieve pressure while in other cases, part of the core of the limb was removed to allow the branch to take a sharper bend.

Today, arbor sculp-
turorists have ex-
panded the art form
of deforming a tree
to create almost any
shape   imaginable.
These shapes are creat-
ed by wounding parts
of a tree including re-
moval of parts of the
cambium layer and
then binding these
parts together to cre-
ate new shapes. The
newly shaped tree has
to be supported for a

Figure 4-1 Arbor-Sculpture

long time so that it can heal and have strength enough to hold
the new shape such as seen in Figure 4-1.

Through artful pruning, the arbor sculpture can be guided
into the desired shape. A prune cut above a leaf or node can
steer the plant. If a leaf points to the right, then a cut above
that leaf will produce new growth that grows to the right side.
Likewise, a cut above a leaf pointing to the left produces new
growth that grows to the left.

Through the development of bonsai and arborsculpture, ar-
borists have learned to manipulate plant tissue to create deformed trees. It is quite possible that Indians had learned some
of these techniques and through experimentation had perfected the art of bending trees into the various shapes seen today.

Basic Bending of a Tree

Most authors have reported and or speculated that a tree
was bent as shown in the Figure 4-2. This way of bending
the tree appears to be confirmed in Laura Hubler's drawing
(Figure 4-9) of a bent tree based on what she learned from a
Blackfoot Indian.

Figure 4-2 Bending tree horizontal

For the most common bent trees, it was believed a yoke stick was placed against the bottom of the tree a foot of more above the ground and the tree was bent around the yoke until the tree was essentially horizontal to the ground. The tree was held in that position using a rope made from animal hides or other parts of the animal. The tree would have to remain in this position for perhaps a year in order to be deformed to that shape.

During the time the tree was tied down, it would require maintenance to remove all unwanted limbs that began to grow vertically. Usually, one limb near the end of the horizontal bend would be allowed to grow vertically to create the marker tree. After this limb had begun to grow sufficiently, the remaining section of the horizontal trunk would be cut off or allowed to atrophy and drop off *(see Figure 4-3)*. After this had happened, the nose section could be fashioned into whatever shape was desired.

Figure 4-3 Horizontal Member Cut

For some trees it is likely that the vertical portion of the marker tree was bent from the main trunk by bending the trunk horizontal and then pulling the remaining trunk back to vertical as depicted in Figure 4-4. This must have been harder to accomplish requiring the tree to be bent into an "S" shape and held there for a long time.

Bending a tree causes major changes in the cambium layer which is the life-blood of the tree. The cambium layer located just inside the inter-bark layer is a few molecules thick and provides all the nutrients for the tree growth. When the tree is bent, the cambium layer is stretched on the outer part of the bent and crushed on the interior bend. This certainly has a disrup- tive affect to the tree

Figure 4-4 "S" Bent Tree

growth. This is similar to when a tree is scarred with removal of a section of bark including the cambium layer. The tree will repair the damage of the scar by growing bark to cover it but the cambium layer must spiral around the scar to keep nutri- ents flowing to the tree. Most likely the amount of nutrients is somewhat reduced. If the tree is scarred completely around the trunk losing the cambium layer, then the tree will die.

When one studies the horizontal bends of the trees, it is obvious that the tree has been bent into an almost 90 degree bend. This is very difficult to do without breaking the trunk unless something unknown to us was done to the tree to make it more flexible. It is more likely that the outer skin of the tree at the bend was cut laterally to relieve the tension on the tree as shown in Figure 4-5.

Figure 4-5 "S" Possible Method of Relieving Fiber Stress

The tree fi- bers or strands that grow axially in the tree are in- creasingly in high- er tension as you move radially out from the tree cen- ter. If the tension exceeds the tensile limits of these fibers, then the tree will split. To avoid the tree splitting, the outer fibers most likely have to be cut or a small amount of tree fibers removed to lessen the tensile force in the fibers. This is exactly how the bonsai trees are

bent and quite possibly how arbor sculpture is created. Figure 4-6 shows an existing trail tree hip section that is commonly found on the trees. The hole or slit section on the outer layer of the tree is

Figure 4-6 Trail Tree Hip

most likely caused by removing material or slitting the tree at the hip to allow it to be bent into the 90 degree position. The tree easily heals itself from this cut and leaves the scar on the hip of the tree. In some cases, however, the disturbed hip section leaves a hole in the tree which allows water to enter into the tree which may affect the longevity of the tree.

Some trees believed to be Indian trail trees have been found as shown in Figure 4-7 which have a larger section of the outer part of the bend removed. It is believed that some trees were bent later in their life beyond the sapling stage thus requiring more material to be removed to form the tree in order for it be bent or deformed. As can be seen in Figure 4-7, the tree appears to have been split axially along the outer part of the bend and material removed. Over time the scar healed itself leaving an indented surface on the tree.

Figure 4-8 shows a hip section of a trail tree where the hip scar did not heal over, allowing water to enter the tree and causing damage to the tree. The damage to the tree usually is the cause for the tree to eventually die. However, in the case of the tree in Figure 4-8 the tree has lived through this rotting out of the core of the tree and the cambium layer has obviously sustained

Figure 4-7 Trail Tree with Large Hip Scar

the tree even though greatly impaired.

The nose section of a trail tree was probably also modified by the Indians. Laura Hubler, in her pioneering work on trail trees in 1975, drew the diagram shown in Figure 4-9. Based on her research with the Blackfeet and Choctaw Indians, it is believed she learned how the nose section was formed. Her diagram indicates

Figure 4-8 Hip Section Rotting

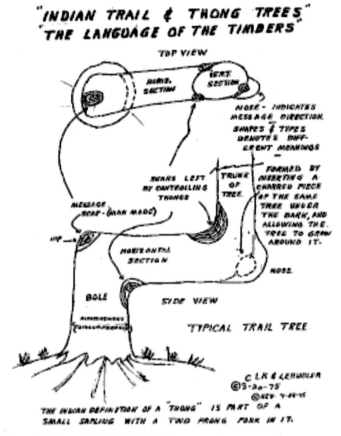

Figure 4-9 Laura Hubler's Trail Tree Diagram circa 1975

that the bark on the nose of the pointer was probably opened and either a charred piece of wood or possibly moss was placed there and the bark allowed to grow around it. Most of the nose sections of the trees that have been located either show a smooth closing of the nose wound by the bark growing over it or they show what appears to be some manipulation of the nose to form characteristic shapes. In some rare cases, the nose has the appearance of a face.

Figure 4-10 shows what might be called a typical nose of a trail tree. The majority of trail trees have the rounded nose but it is not uncommon to find variations in the formation of each nose. It is speculated that the nose was formed after the vertical limb adjacent to the nose area had begun to grow and gotten well established. Once the vertical limb began to grow, the horizontal section of the tree, just after the limb, was ei-

Figure 4-10 Typcial Trail Tree Nose Section

ther cut off or allowed to atrophy.

No all trail trees have rounded noses, and in fact there may be hundreds of variations based on what has been found across the nation. Figure 4-11 shows

Figure 4-11 Long Nose Trail Tree

a variation of nose section wherein the horizontal section has been allowed to remain well past the vertical member. This may have been done to enhance the pointer configuration of the tree. A slight variation to the long nose is one that is shorter in length with some rounding at the end of the nose as seen in Figure 4-12.

Figure 4-12 Extended Long Nose Variation

The nose on some trees is very pointed and small which possibly indicates that the horizontal section of the tree was formed with the vertical section creating a small nose section. Figure 4-13 shows one of the unique trail trees that has a pointed nose

as well as an oval shape. This tree may have been shaped by bending the tree into an "S" shape and using the trunk to form both the horizontal and vertical section of the tree.

Figure 4-13

Another variation of the trail tree nose can be seen in Figure 4-14. A number of the discovered trail trees have a deep angular bend toward the ground. On these type trees the vertical section of the tree has to be bent back beyond a vertical angle causing the nose section to be formed from the horizontal and vertical parts of the tree. In Figure 4-14, the nose is somewhat rounded but also blended into the tree configuration.

The deep pointer tree is one that is commonly found throughout the nation. The reason for the deeper bend is unknown but it usually approximates a forty-five degree angle. Some of these type trees may be associated with pointing toward water or shelter.

Figure 4-14 Deep Pointer Nose

The Unique Trail Tree Noses

While most of the nose sections on the discovered Trail Trees are either of the rounded or long-pointer noses, there are some whose characteristics are very different. These noses surely required more skill to create than the normally found trees.

Figure 4-15 shows the simplest of the unique noses which is a flat nose. It would appear that some hard object was jammed against the nose to force it to grow out in a flattened shape.

Another variation that is seen often is noses with various appurtenances added to the nose as a symbol with some possible special meaning. Figure 4-16 shows a typical tree with the nose

Figure 4-15 Flat Nose

manipulated into a particular symbolic shape.

The most unique noses are the ones that have the appearance of what might be considered an animal face. Some nose sections for a Trail Tree appear to look like a deer while others have been found that look like a bear. In Figure 4-17, the tree face almost appears to look like a cow or similar animal.

Figure 4-18 shows another tree with an animal characteristic. This tree has two appurtenances wherein eyes and the nose have been shaped to add to the animal appearance.

Figure 4-16 Nose Appurtenances

Up close, this tree looks like a rhino head however; the Indians didn't encounter rhinos from what we know of their history.

Figure 4-17 Animal face Trail Tree

The strangest trees found with possible facial appearances are ones with long snout noses as seen in Figure 4-19. This tree might be expected to be found in an arbor sculptor's business location, but it was found deep in the forest in Georgia. The appurtenances at the bend in the tree have obviously been added by the person who bent the tree to lend a characteristic shape to the tree.

TYPES OF BENT TREES

Figure 4-18 Nose with Animal Characteristics

The variety of bent trees is large with little understanding as to what the meaning of each type may have conveyed to the Indians. Perhaps, there were different styles that existed taught by a particular tribe. Also, different tree benders may have had their own unique style that conveyed meaning to those who had an understanding of that type tree. In one part of Georgia, a number of bent trees have been found in close proximity to each other with uniquely different shapes possibly indicating the trees were bent by different people using their own styles to bend the trees.

Figure 4-19 Animal-like Nose Section

The shapes of the discovered trail trees have been grouped into several categories and discussed in the following paragraphs.

Common Horizontal Bent Tree

Probably the most common Trail Tree is the one with a horizontal bent member and one vertical member located at the end of the horizontal member forming what is commonly called a pointer or marker tree. These trees are typically bent close to the ground but vary from a foot to as much as six feet. Figure 4-20 shows a common horizontal tree bent low to the ground and Figure 4-21 shows one bent higher off the ground.

One of the main characteristics of the horizontally bent trees as well as with some of the other types is the changes in the overall shape of the trunk. Bending the tree puts a lot of stress on the tree fibers to make the 90-degree bend at the hip and then again at the vertical member. The tree may start out in a round configuration typical of most trees but the stresses of the bend seem to cause the tree to change to a more oval shape.

The width of the tree trunk is much larger perpendicular to the tree as compared to linearly along the axis of the tree. This may be the result of the cambium layer

Figure 4-20 Common Horizontal Bent Tree

having to stretch to accommodate the bend or from other causes as the tree adjusts to an unnatural shape into

Figure 4-21 Horizontal Bent Tree

which it has been forced. Figures 4-22 and Figure 4-23 show the changing of the tree shape from round to oval as it goes through the bending process. Above the bend for the vertical member, the tree changes back to a round shape.

Figure 4-24 shows some of the typical affects of the bending stresses on a tree. As the tree transitions from the round trunk to the horizontal bend at the hip, the tree appears to be compensating for the bend by stretching the shape to oval and tries to fill in under the bend to support the now cantilevered horizontal section. Again, as the tree is bent to form the vertical member, the tree has to compensate for the added stress and fills in the inside of the bend. The filling in process seems to be the cause for the tree to neck down at the bends. This may be the result of the cambium layer stretching to make the turn and to keep nutrients flowing to the tree.

This is exactly what is done in the engineering of bridge trusses wherein gusset plates

Figure 4-22 Oval Shape of Bent Tree

and other structure members are added to the beam to accommodate the added stresses from transitioning from a vertical

Figure 4-23 Oval Shape of Bent Tree

member to a horizontal member. The added material also allows the joint to accommodate the moment forces from the cantilever section. Figure 4-25 shows a cantilever bridge section with the added structural material to accommodate the stresses.

One of the variations of the common horizontal bent tree is what is referred to as the "S" bent tree (see Figure 4-26). These trees have almost no horizontal section and appear to have been bent from vertical to vertical with a slight jog in the vertical axis. These trees typically are oval in shape which is undoubtedly due to the bending stresses the tree is experiencing. It accom-

Figure 4-24 Tree Bending Stress Effects

modates those stresses by growing into an oval shape by filling in at the bend area.

Another variation of the horizontally bent tree is the placement of the vertical member. Most of these trees have the vertical member at the end of the horizontal section. However, some trees have the vertical member back from the end of the horizontal section, thus accommodating a longer nose section. Figure 4-27 shows a tree

Figure 4-25 Cantilever Bridge Section

with the vertical member other than at the end.

Horizontal Marker Tree Uses

Figure 4-26 "S" Bent Tree

The commonly found horizontal marker trees are believed to have been used primarily to mark trails, water, shelter and possible medicinal sites. Before the culture of the Indians changed, they traveled great distances to hunt and gather, and to communicate with other segments of their tribal brethren.

In north Georgia where the trees were first discovered by our group, it was determined through the use of Geographic Information Systems (GIS) technology and topographic maps that the trees found on a ridge line were aligned along an old trail.

Figure 4-27 Vertical Member Variation

The trail was at one point in the 1930-1950s part of the Appalachian Trail. Before that time, it appears that it was an Indian trail leading from a small Cherokee village uphill to the ridgeline and then heading north along the ridgeline to a major Cherokee town and district some 25 miles north. The Appalachian Trail followed this same ridgeline for approximately half the distance to the Cherokee towns to the north before heading northeast. The trees that are along this ridge appear to align perfectly to map the old trail. Figure 4-28 shows a Google Earth image of a few of the located trees highlighted in yellow along the suspected trail.

Figure 4-28 Trail Trees Marking Old Indian Trail

Figure 4-29   Marker Trees Leading to Water

The trees were initially found by locating the first tree and then following a compass bearing of the pointer to locate the next tree in the alignment. This technique has been used extensively in the tree search across the nation resulting in other trees being located nearby. The fact that the tree, in some cases, points to the next tree along a trail confirms that these trees were used to mark a trail. This was also confirmed by the writings of some of the early scholars who studied the trees reported in Chapter 2.

The Indians that made long treks along these trails needed to know, in particular, where water was located to refresh themselves and to restock. Some of the pointer trees were used to guide the Indians to springs or small streams. In the area in Georgia where the trail and marker trees are located, there are at least thirty to forty springs just over the side of the ridgeline where an Indian could go to find water and in some cases shelter. Figure 4-29 shows one example of trees leading downhill to several spring sites. In the Google Earth image, the marker trees are shown in yellow and are aligned downhill from the trail location which was to the right of the ridge road.

Figure 4-30 Marker Tree at Shallow Ford

Another example of the use of a marker tree is to mark the location of a shallow ford stream crossing. When a stream had to be forded, the Indians always knew where to cross avoiding those areas of the stream that were dangerous. A number of the trees that have been found appear to be marking the stream crossings. Some are located at the shallow ford and others have been found that point downhill to where the ford crossing is located

In Figure 4-30, one of two located marker trees was used to point to the shallow ford crossing on the Chattooga River in South Carolina. The Indian trail associated with this crossing can also be located on either side of the stream.

COMMON TREE WITH VERTICAL VARIATIONS

To the Indian who could read the signs of the trail or marker tree, there was a message in the tree. In some cases it provided information on the direction of the trail or possibly to a water or shelter location off of the trail. But some trees had other messages either associated with the overall shape, the nose or possibly associated with the number of vertical members the tree had. It is well known that some Cherokees disappeared off of the Trail of Tears during removal. It is believed that they may have been reading the signs of the trees along the trail and knew where to walk away.

Ralph Jenkins of Temple University did research on the Trail of Tears detachments that made the trip to Oklahoma. His research shows that there were 1,301 Cherokees that disappeared from the trail.[51] Some probably died along the trail, other perhaps turned back while still others stayed where they left and began a new life.

Multiple Vertical Members

The majority of trees found with more than one vertical member have two. However several have three and on rare occasions, a tree can be found with four vertical members. Figure 4-31 shows a typical marker tree with two vertical members. In the case of the two vertical member trees, the verticals are usually one at the end of the horizontal member and another somewhere along the horizontal member but not at the hip which is another variation to discuss next.

Figure 4-32 and Figure 4-33 show two examples of trees with four verticals. The number of verticals probably signifies some meaning but it is not known. The

Figure 4-31 Horizontal Marker Tree with Two Verticals

tree in Figure 4-32 is located at a possible trail junction point with the four members probably associated with the change in direction of the trail. The tree in Figure 4-33 in on the trail previously mentioned in Georgia.

Horizontal Member Created from Branch or Trunk

A variation of the two vertical members is one where the first vertical at the hip is the main trunk of the tree and the horizontal member has been created from a low branch growing near the bottom of the tree. For most cases, it is believed this horizontal member was a natu-

Figure 4-32 Four Verticals

Figure 4-33 Four Verticals

rally growing branch on the tree or perhaps it was forced to grow by some horticultural effect on the tree. There is one other way to have a branch grow at the bottom of the tree and that is to graft a branch to the trunk.

There are no written accounts that indicate the Indians knew how to graft a branch to a tree. However, there are a number of trees that have been found wherein there is no way a particular branch on the tree could have grown in its position without grafting. Figure 4-34 shows how a branch can be grafted to a tree trunk. This is not a difficult process and probably was known to the Indians.

There are three variations of Trail and Marker Trees where the trunk plays a role in one of the vertical members. Figure 4-35 shows a tree created with the main trunk serving as the hori-

Figure 4-34 Technique for Grafting Limb to Tree Trunk

zontal and end vertical and a secondary trunk growing vertical from the hip area. It is impossible to determine if the hip vertical was grafted to the main trunk or something was done to make a branch grow at that point. As can be seen in the picture, the branch covers a large portion of the hip area. In the central plains states, this type tree configuration is called a thong tree.

A second alternative to this configuration is where the main trunk of the tree is the first vertical member and a smaller branch has either been grafted onto the trunk or allowed to grow to form the horizontal and second vertical member of the tree. Figure 4-36 shows an example tree of this type configuration.

A third variation of this type tree is

Figure 4-35 Hip Vertical from Secondary Trunk or Branch

where the main trunk of the tree may have been modified to add a second member which then became the horizontal and second vertical. The horizontal member appears to be an integral part of the main trunk of the tree with the second vertical member growing off of the horizontal member. The tree in Figure 4-37 is located in central Arkansas. The owner of the property where the tree is located said the old timers told him it was an Indian tree and it pointed

Figure 4-36 Thong Tree with Branch Horizontal Member

to a spring located near the tree.[26]

The tree examples shown in Figures 4-35 – 4-37 have been characteristically named *four* trees because their shape is like the

Figure 4-37 Thong Tree with Large Integral Trunk and Horizontal

number four. A large number of trees have been found that exhibit this shape characteristic, some with prominent noses and others with simpler noses.

One last point about the creation of the four trees is that some may have been created by grafting two trees together. Figure 4-38 shows a four tree with an axial indention in the center of the trunk possibly indicating that two trees were forced to grow together with one becoming the first vertical and the second one being bent to form the horizontal member and the second vertical.

LARGE BENT TREES

Figure 4-38 Four Tree Created from Two Trees

Less common of the trees that have been described so far are the large bent trees that seem to defy gravity and fiber stress caused by the bending of the tree. Some of these type trees have the single vertical member at the end of the horizontal and other take on the appearance of being a *goal post*. Figure 4-39 shows a tree that has been bent creating a very long span. The horizontal span on this tree from the hip to the vertical is 15 feet with a diameter of 4 feet and a 10 foot circumference. The moment force on the trunk of this tree required to hold the tree upright must be significant. It's a wonder the tree remains standing today.

Observe how the tree is transitioning from the horizontal to the vertical. The tree appears to have grown layers of fibers outwardly from the vertical bend to support the weight and stresses of the long span tree.

Very few of these large trees are found today in the forests possibly because the weight and stress caused by long span has toppled the tree; however, trees with small diameter trunks have been found as seen in Figure 4-40.

Figure 4-41 shows a variation of the long span trail tree that is commonly called the *goal post* tree. This type configuration may have the function as serving as a boundary marker tree.

Figure 4-39 Long Span Trail Tree

Boundary Marker Trees

Figure 4-40 Long Span Tree

Figure 4-42 shows a tree located in the Bankhead National Forest in Alabama which is believed to have been a boundary marker tree. This tree is also located near the site of a major battle between the Creek and Chickasaw Indians. The tree may be marking the battle site and it may also mark where those that died in the battle are buried. It is one of the most unique trees that

Figure 4-41 Goal Post Tree

have been located. Like some of the four trees, it appears to have been created by planting two trees together and grafting them into one trunk to create boundary marker shape.

The remaining trees to be discussed are what might be categorized as *special purpose* trees. These trees have more unusual characteristics and were associated with a particular message which for the most part is unknown today.

ANGULAR BENT TREE

The angular bent trees are not as commonly found as those previously discussed; thus, they may have a special purpose. The upwardly bent trees appear, for

Figure 4-42 Boundary Marker Tree

the most part, to have been bent from a single tree trunk without having to nurture a vertical limb to grow to complete the pointer. The downwardly bent trees, on the other hand, usually have a vertical limb either grafted on to the bent section, or the person bending the tree has nurtured a vertical limb to grow on the bent section.

Figure 4-43 shows a typically upward bent tree. The nose on these trees is usually smaller since the angular member is also the vertical member. However, the nose on this type tree distinguishes it from a tree that had been bent due to another tree falling on it. For those trees the angular bend of the tree is rounded without any nose indicating a natural bend.

The downwardly bent angular trees are somewhat unusual in that they must have taken a lot more skill to create. The downward angle is usually around 45 degrees creating a member that is pointing at the ground near the base of the tree. The

stresses on the
sapling to bend
the tree approx-
imately 135 de-
grees from ver-
tical had to be
enormous. Un-
doubtedly, re-
moval of core
material or split-
ting the out-
er bend had to
be done to allow
the tree to make
this sharp a bend
without splitting
the tree.

Figure 4-43 Upwardly Bent Tree

While many of the downwardly bent angular trees are either 45 degrees or less in their bent configuration, some have
been found that are bent almost 180 degrees which defies an
explanation on how it was done. Figure 4-45 shows a tree in
Georgia that has been bent about 180 degrees with a vertical
member nurtured to grow vertical from the end of the bent
section which appears to have been cut off flat.

The tree in Figure 4-44 is in north Georgia near the site of
an Indian village. The tree points away from the site. Another
bent tree is located near this tree and there are at least 40 other
bent trees near this tree within a 5 mile radius.

The tree in Figure 4-45 is also in north Georgia and is located just above a small stream and waterfall. The tree is probably
indicating that water is nearby and possibly the sharper bend
is related to the existence of the waterfall.

WATER MARKER TREES

Figure 4-44 Downward Bent Angular Tree

When the trail trees began to be found in north Georgia along the old Indian Trail, one tree configuration kept being found. In fact, approximately 20 of these trees were found within a 25 mile radius. Each time one of these trees was found, a spring was located within several hundred feet of the tree. These oddly shaped *snout* trees have been found with two eyes, one eye and no eyes in the snout. The eyes must

Figure 4-45 Angular Tree Bent Almost 180 Degrees

signify something but that is not understood. What is understood, though, is this type tree seems to signify the availability of water nearby.

After discovering these type trees in Georgia, they were also found in many other eastern and Great Plains states and they seem to also indicate the availability of water. Based on a large number of these trees being found throughout the nation, it has been determined that the meaning of this tree configuration is water. The meaning of the eyes in the snout may be related to the size of the water source. One tree near a larger stream has two eyes and one near a smaller spring has one eye. Figure 4-46 shows a typical snout tree.

DOUBLETS

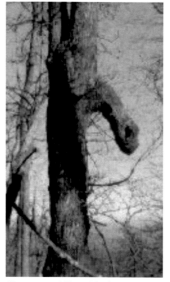

One of the most unusal trees located across the nation are called the *doublets*. These trees are rare but undoubtedly have some very special meaning. One of the doublets is located near the Eastern Band of the Cherokee Indian Qualla Boundary in North Carolina. The other doublet was found in Barry County, Missouri. These trees are most definitely bent by man as the odds of two trees being located within a few feet of each other and being bent identical is astronomical.

Figure 4-46 Water Marker

One interesting aspect about the North Carolina doublets is that one of the trees is an oak tree and the other is a beech tree. These two trees are on the side of an old road on a rather steep hill. What they appear to be pointing to is unknown but there is a small stream near the bottom of the hill. Figure 4-47 shows the Missouri Double Trees and Figure 4-48 the North Carolina Doublets.

UNUSUAL BENT TREES

Speculation and hypothesis of the tree bending methods and techniques of the previously shown trees is within our mental capacity. However, for these next trail and marker tree types, logical conclusions on how the tree was created fail us. These are what we will

Figure 4-47 Missouri Doublet Trees

call the very un-
usual trees.

Figure 4-49
shows an exam-
ple marker tree
that has a live
branch grow-
ing through the
center of the
tree to act as
the pointer. It is
speculated that
a hole had to be
opened through

Figure 4-48 North Carolina Doublets

the sapling and the branch grafted into the main trunk. With
time the ends of the branch were cut off to form the pointer.
This tree is located on a site in Georgia where there are 17 trail/
marker trees and where evidence of the Cherokees living on or
near the site has been discovered.

Figure 4-49 Horizontal Branch Through Tree

A type of tree sim-
ilar to the tree in Fig-
ure 4-49 is one with
a branch growing
through the horizon-
tal member of the tree
at an angle. An ex-
ample of these type
trees is shown in Fig-
ure 4-50 and 4-51.
On these trees, there
appears to have been
a branch inserted
through the tree to

form the angular member. Alternatively, the large nose section
could have been formed normally and an appurtenance added to the other side of the nose to form what appears to be the
other side of the branch. Regardless of methodology used, it's a

very unusual tree shape whose meaning is unclear.

Another example of the tree within a tree is shown in Figure 4-52. This example tree is located in Arkansas where a large number of Indian artifacts

Figure 4-50 Angular Branch Through Trunk

have been found. How this tree was created defies all explanation.

Figure 4-51 Angular Branch Through
Horizontal Member

The tree in Figure 4-52 appears to have a tree growing through the bent tree. It is speculated that the main bent tree was somehow opened to allow another tree branch to grow through the main trunk to form the angular pointer. It is also quite possible that a branch was

grafted onto the hip and then forced to grow at the exact angle of the bent section, thus making the tree appear as if another tree is growing through it. Also strange about this tree is that the two vertical members appear to have been either grafted to the side of the tree or have been cultured to have grown from that position. This is quite possibly the strangest tree found to date and it is thought to have some very special meaning as-

Figure 4-52 Unusual Trail Tree

sociated with the possible Indian site where it is located.

Figure 4-53 is similar to the trees with angular members except this type tree seems have been bent in an animal characteristic shape. As can be seen in the insert, the angular member on the tree hip has the shape possibly like ears. Also the nose is flattened and just below the vertical member and to the left appears to be an eye. The existence of an eye shape in a tree would generally be dismissed as being caused by some abnormal growth. However, searching through the database of trail trees in the thousands covering 39 states, one can find a large number of cases where the tree appears to have an eye shape in the tree. Figure 4-54 shows one more of the many trees that have been found that have the eye shape on the tree. This tree is located in Arkansas along the Old Military Route which is also known as the Bell Trail of Tears Route.

One last type of unusual trees could be categorized as those with very strange bends that seem to test the trees capability to sustain forces that exceed the tensile

Figure 4-53 Unusual Trail Tree

Figure 4-54 Tree with Eye Shape on Bell Trail of Tears Route

strength of the fibers. There is no pattern to these trees and each one is unique. Figure 4-55 shows just one of these type trees. This tree found in Arkansas has a large bulbous area at the bend from horizontal to vertical plus it has what appears to be a grafted member to the bulbous section. The added weight at the end of the cantilever section of the tree is obviously putting a stain on the base of the tree. Figure 4-56 is another example of an unusually bent tree also found in Arkansas. This tree defies all logic as to how it was bent into the shape as seen in the figure.

APPURTANCE TREES

With the loss of the tribal elders and their teaching the Indian culture to the younger generations, the meaning of the various shaped bent trees has been in all probability lost. With that

Figure 4-55 Unusual Trail Tree

loss is also the mean-
ing of the added ap-
purtenances to the
trees which were in
all likelihood *a mes-
sage on a message.* The
appurtenance trees
have seemingly vari-
ous shapes added to
them to spell out an
additional message
to the Indians that
passed by the tree.
For the most part,
the added shapes are

Figure 4-56 Unusual Trail Tree

growths that were created in specific locations on the tree sometimes in patterns and sometimes as individual shapes. Trees with
the added appurtenances have been found mostly in the southern and plains states.

Figure 4-57 shows a tree which has a square pattern of
bumps on the hip section of the tree. A few of these type trees
have been found. Figure 4-58 shows another example of a hip
appurtenance which is made up of 3-4 bumps added that together look like a crown.

Two other examples
of trees with the add-
ed bumps on the tree
were found in Arkan-
sas. One of these trees,
Figure 4-59 has eight
bumps on the outer
bend of the tree which
are aligned in pairs of
two's on the bend of the
tree. Note that this tree
also appears to have

Figure 4-57 Square Pattern Appurtenances

two eyes on the tree. The second tree has a similar configuration of the bumps however there are fifteen of them in somewhat of a snake pattern. This tree is shown in Figure 4-60.

Figure 4-58 Tree with Hip Appurtenance

In Georgia, 3 trees were located within a 5 mile radius, each of which had the exact same appurtenance on the tree at the exact same spot on the outer bend of the tree. One of these trees is shown in Figure 4-61 with the appurtenance located in the center of the bend of the tree. All of these trees have the same angular downward bend.

The last example of the appurtenances trees are those with unique noses sections. The tree in Figure 4-62 is located in Alabama near an old Indian Trail and a possible Indian camp site that was also a chipping site since a lot of arrowhead have been located at that the site. The tree points directly to the site. The nose on this tree seems to have some appurtenances which possibly have added meaning the tree shape.

TRAIL/MARKER TREES CREATED FROM PINES TREES

Initially, pine trees were discounted as being a possible Indian Trail/Marker Tree. Based on engineering calculations, the allowable fiber stresses in bending for White Pine is 1,000 pounds per square inch and 1,500 pounds per square inch for yellow pine. This is compared to white oak which is about 2.5 times stronger. One only has to visit a forested area after a major wind storm

Figure 4-59 Tree with Eight Bumps and Eyes

Figure 4-60 Fifteen Bump Tree

where there are hundreds of pines blown over and splintered to begin to discount pines as a viable species for being bent as a trail tree.

However, after visiting the sites of a lot of similarly bent pine trees in the southeast and in the Plains states, it became obvious that the Indians had learned how to relieve enough of the stresses in a pine tree to allow it to be bent at 90 degree angles and more. Based on observations of the hip area on these trees, it appears some amount of core material was removed from the tree to allow it to be bent.

Figure 4-61 Triangular Appurtenance on Georgia Tree

Figure 4-63 shows a loblolly pine tree that has been bent at a 90 degree angle. At the bent portion of the tree, a concave area can be seen where core material from the tree was probably removed to allow the tree to be bent. Figure 4-64 shows another bent pine in the configuration of the typical trail tree.

Some of the bent pines have special shapes that probably had a particular meaning to the Indians but that meaning is lost today. Figure 4-65 is one example of these specially bent pine trees.

Chapter 6 will show examples of bent Ponderosa Pines that were used by the Ute Indians and other western tribes.

Figure 4-62 Tree with Unique Nose

Figure 4-63 Bent Loblolly Pine Tree

Figure 4-64 Pine Bent Like Typical Trail Tree

Figure 4-65 Specially Bent Pine Tree

Chapter 5

WITNESS TREES AND INDIGENOUS SYMBOLOGY

Before we can talk about witness trees and their symbology, we must first talk about the symbology of the indigenous peoples.

Symbols have been carved or chipped into rocks, cave walls and on structural walls for hundreds of thousand years. The pictures, or symbols, that were used are fascinating. The earliest examples of human communication are found in this rock art. Based on the Greek words for stone, petra, and to carve, glyhein, these ancient art forms are called petroglyphs. Another form of rock art, pictographs, appeared much later than petroglyphs. Pictographs are painted rather than carved on the rocks. Perhaps because it was more difficult to carve or chip designs into rock, there are many more pictographs than petroglyphs. Petroglyphs also tend to be symbolic and representational while pictographs are more realistic. Figure 5-1 shows a petroglyph

Figure 5-1 Petroglyph

US FISH AND WILDLIFE SERVICE, ZUNI INDIAN RESERVATION, NM

from the Zuni Indian-Reservation in New Mexico.

In the 1990s a discovery was made that caused scientists to rethink the age of petroglyphs. Petroglyphs were discovered in two ancient quartzite caves in India that are believed to date to at least 290,000 BCE! It is possible that they are even older than that. Most petroglyphs and pictographs are found in India, Africa, Scandinavia, Siberia, Australia and North Ameri-

ca. In fact, they are found in all parts of the world except Ant-
arctica. Pictographs are believed to date as far back as 10,000
years.

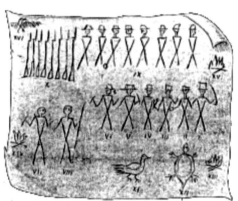

Figure 5-2 Indian Pictogtraph

More recent-
ly, though, the
American Indi-
ans have used
pictographs to
tell their sto-
ries. Figure 5-2
shows an Indian
pictograph that
was reported by
Henry School-
craft from one
of his expeditions in 1820.[52] Schoolcraft and fifteen others
were exploring the Great Lakes regions with Indian guides.
On one morning when they awoke at their camp, one of the
Indian guides had created the diagram in Figure 5-2. The eight
figures at the top of the tree bark scroll represent the soldiers
on the trip. The six figures below the soldiers are Schoolcraft's
party including himself, a geologist, a scribe, an interpreter,
and several others. The two figures in the lower left are the
Chippewa Indian guides. In the upper left are the muskets of
the soldiers and the lower right depicts food that they ate. This
scroll was placed on a tall stick and bent to point in the direction of their travel so that other Indians passing by could tell
the story of their group and where they were heading.

The paint was made from pulverized minerals. Red, black,
and white were the most common colors, but sometimes other colors were created as well. Pictographs used symbols that
resembled what they signified. They were the basis for cunei-
form writing and Egyptian hieroglyphs. Pictograms are still in
use today as well. For example, while walking in a shopping
center, you look up to see very stylized symbols of a man and
a woman; you know immediately that these indicate a public

restroom. Or, while driving, you see a yellow sign with a picture of a black truck headed downhill; you know that you are approaching a steep grade.

Native American rock art is thousands of years old. It was probably created for many reasons – aesthetic, religious, magical, astronomical, ritual, and more. An estimated 30,000 petroglyphs can be found in Arizona, New Mexico, Colorado and Utah. Texas, California and Nevada have fewer known sites. Many of the sites are protected areas open to the public. There are many more unprotected sites. Some of these sites have been desecrated by vandals and those hunting for examples that can be sold on the black market.

Trying to interpret all of the symbols is difficult to impossible. When outsiders try to interpret them, it is important that they be aware of their lack of knowledge. For instance, when scholars first attempted to decipher Egyptian hieroglyphics they believed that the intricate characters represented whole ideas. They found it impossible to believe that the hieroglyphics represented phonetic characters. They were certain that the idea of phonetic spelling was too complex for such an ancient civilization. They were wrong. Eventually the discovery of the Rosetta Stone, which had the same message in hieroglyphics, Greek and demotic, would enable scholars to decipher that fascinating form of Egyptian writing.

With passing generations and changing cultures, some meanings that might have been known probably changed. A symbol adopted by one tribe from another tribe may well have acquired a totally different meaning. Meanings placed on symbols by modern scholars may continue to be as far from the mark as the early effort to decipher the Rosetta Stone. Some scholars believe that symbols found in Rock Art were almost always religious in nature. However, it seems that some may well have been directional marks placed along a trail, while others pointed the way to water or another natural feature. They may have been used to mark territory or identify a specific tribe or clan. Art carved into or painted onto rock was not

the only place American Indian symbols were used. Beautiful-
ly beaded wampum belts, clothing, pottery, basketry, sticks,
cedar bark and buffalo hides all had their share of the designs.

When the Spanish began to move into the area of the
northern hemisphere, they added their own rock art. Their
art, probably created by explorers, traders, settlers, sheepherd-
ers, missionaries or soldiers, included Christian crosses and in-
scriptions. As settlers moved west towards Oregon and California, rock art went with them. They frequently left their
names and the date of their passing on landmark rocks along
the trails. Perhaps spray painted graffiti on the concrete *rocks*
of a highway overpass is a modern equivalent.

Many of us learned to remember the names of the Great
Lakes by using the mnemonic HOMES – Huron, Ontario,
Michigan, Erie and Superior. Indigenous people in America
also used a form of mnemonic to help them remember their
complex history, culture, and stories as well as to keep track
of the passing of years. Since Native Americans did not have a
written language, remembering their history was very important. Accurate information had to be passed from one generation to another. Symbols and pictures were used in creative
ways to help them remember. One use of buffalo hides in the
Great Plains was as a mnemonic tool to help them remember
the winter count. Years, called winters, were measured from
the first snowfall of one year to the first snowfall of the next.
Near the end of each year, the elders would gather and discuss what had happened during that winter. They would de-
cide what event would serve as the reminder for the whole
year. The year was then named after that event and the *Keeper,*
the one chosen to paint the pictographs onto the buffalo hide,
would add that year's symbol to the story.

The hide with all its symbols was known as the winter count.
Just as a photo album might remind us of the events that have
made up our family history, the symbols on the buffalo hide
reminded them of who they were and where they had come
from, and what had happened to them. One well-known winter count documents seventy years (1800-1871) of Yanktonais

Nakota history. The pictograph symbols begin in the center of the hide and spiral outward in a counterclockwise direction. A man named Lone Dog was the last keeper of the account so it is known as the Lone Dog Winter Count. It is a record that illustrates encounters with other native peoples, years when there were wars or epidemics, and other memorable events. You can see the Lone Dog Winter Count at the Museum of Native American Artifacts in Bentonville, Arkansas.

The poet Henry Wadsworth Longfellow was very interested in pictography that he learned from the Indians and from books written by early researchers into Indian history. In his poem *The Song of Hiawatha*, which first appeared in 1855, we can read about some of the symbols.

> *"For the earth he drew a straight line,*
> *For the sky a bow above it;*
> *White the space between for day-time,*
> *Filled with little stars for night-time;*
> *On the left a point for sunrise,*
> *On the right a point for sunset,*
> *On the top a point for noontide,*
> *And for rain and cloudy weather*
> *Waving lines descending from it.*[53]*"

Another form of pictography that is often mentioned is the use of engraved or painted sticks. The most well known is the Walam Olum. The name signifies *painted tally* or *red score*, from walam, *painted*, particularly *red painted*, and *olum*, a score or tally. This is purportedly a historical record of the Lenape (Delaware) Indians. The document has been surrounded with controversy since its publication in the 1830s. Rafinesque, its publisher, claimed that the original was recorded in pictograph on birch bark, cedar wood tablets called sticks. Much debate and archaeological studies have determined that the walam olum is a hoax, although some of it seems to be based on actual Lenape stories.

Twentieth century archeology has confirmed that Native Americans have been using birch bark scrolls for over 400 years. So by Rafinesque's time, trimmed and shaped pieces of birch bark on which figures of animals, birds, men, mythological creatures and odd symbols had been scratched could have been accepted as authentic. The Ojibwa Indians made great use of birch bark scrolls. Figure 5-3 shows an Ojibwa birch bark scroll from *The Midewiwin*, or *Grand Medicine Society of the Ojibwa*" which was published in Smithsonian Institution, *U.S. Bureau of Ethnology Report*, v. 7, by Walter James Hoffman in 1891.[54]

Sign Language Symbology

Having discussed many ways in which information was passed on from generation to generation by some form of writing, it seems important to discuss another form of communication that may or may not have predated, but is certainly closely connected to, picture writing. That is the Native American sign language. There seems to be some relationship between a thought expressed without words by signs and a thought expressed without words by pictures. Gestures and positions are seen in picture writings that seem to correspond to signs used almost universally by Native Americans. The ancient Indian Sign Language may have been the first uni-

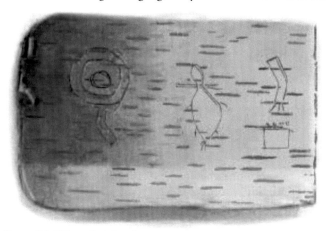

Figure 5-3 Ojibwa Bark Scroll

versal language produced by any people. Many believe that it originated in Mexico and gradually worked its way north. The Plains Indians developed and perpetuated the language to such an extent that it has commonly been called the sign language of the Plains Indians.

Garrick Mallery, Smithsonian Institute, Bureau of Ethnology wrote a book, *Sign Languages Among the North American Indians*,[55] and published it on the internet. Figure 5-4 means,

"I Am Going Home"

(1) Touch the breast with the extended index — *I*, (2) then pass it in a downward curve, outward and upward toward the right nearly to arm's length, as high as the shoulder — *am going (to)*, (3)

Figure 5-4 Indian Sign Language for I Am Going Home

and when at that point suddenly clinch the hand and throw it edgewise a short distance toward the ground —*my country, my home*.

All of the records about the landing of Columbus in 1492 describe how they were able to communicate with the native people by signs. In *Coronado's Journal*, 1540, he says that the Tonkawa or Comanche were very intelligent, that they were able to communicate by means of signs and make themselves understood so well that there was no need for an interpreter. The journals and reports of other explorers echo these sentiments.

Ruxton, in his *Adventurers in Mexico and the Rocky Mountains* (New York, 1848)[56] said,

> *"The language of signs is so perfectly understood in the western country, and the Indians themselves are such admirable sign talkers, that, after a little use, no difficulty whatever exists in carrying on a conversation by such a channel; and there are few mountain men who are at a loss in thoroughly understanding and making themselves intelligible by signs alone, although they neither speak or understand a word of the Indian tongue."[56]*

The same signs seem to exist from Hudson Bay to the Gulf of Mexico. This universal sigh language goes a long way toward explaining how tribes from all areas of what is now the United States were able to trade with one another.

WITNESS TREES

Not only did the Native Americans use birch bark scrolls for sharing information, they also carved symbols onto the outside bark of living trees. Lamar and Kathleen Marshall wrote in the WildSouth Magazine in 2007,

> *"Isolated and scattered across the eastern hardwood forests, primarily along watercourses and springs, hidden away, are tens of thousands of venerable beech trees. Hollowed and smooth-muscled, these trees were the preferred palettes and signposts of the American Indians in the Southeast.[57] "*

In the west, the Indians preferred aspens, in the northern United States the birch tree was used and in the Southeast, the beech tree was preferred.

Like the symbols of the petroglyphs and the pictographs, the symbols carved into the trees called arborglyphs are not easily deciphered. Some of the arborglyph symbols are similar to those seen in the earlier Indian carvings. The Indians have forever carved sacred and utilitarian signs and messages in the sleek bark of the trees.

Ted Franklin Belue in *The Hunters of Kentucky: A Narrative History of American's First Far West, 1750-1792,*[58] wrote about the Indians and frontier men who traveled the Warrior Path in Virginia. He said,

> *"Trees were blazed with hieroglyphics to scare off intruders designated passing tribes and celebrated raids and coup counts. Indian warmarks - sketches of forts and villages; half moons, turtles, otters, suns; and slashes for prisoners taken, an "X" equaling one scalp – warriors had gashed into the beeches and smeared vermillion and gunpowder ink.*[58]*"*

Not all of the marks in the trees were drawn to form a symbol. Some were mere slash marks. One story written by James Mooney about slash marks comes from northeastern Georgia:

> *"Among the curiosities of this country was the Chopped Oak, a tree famous in Indian history and in the traditions of the early settlers. This tree stood about 6 miles southeast of Clarkesville, GA and was noted as being the Law Ground, or place of holding company musters and magistrates' courts. According to tradition, the Chopped Oak was a celebrated rendezvous of the Indians in their predatory excursions, it being at a point where a number of trails met. Here their plans of warfare were laid; here the several parties separated; and here, on their return, they awaited each other; and then, in their brief language, the result of their enterprise was stated, and for every scalp taken a gash cut in the tree. If tradition tells the truth and every scar on the blasted oak counts for a scalp, the success of their scouting parties must have been great. This tree was alive a few years since when a young man, possessing all the prejudices of his countrymen, and caring less for the traditions of the Indians than his own revenge, killed the tree by girdling it, that it might be no longer a living monument of the cruelties of the savages. The stump is still standing.*[59]*"*

Figure 5-5 Alabama Arborglyph

Many of the beech witness trees found today are in the southeastern United States probably done by the Cherokee

and Creeks, although some may be Chickasaw or Choctaw in origin. Figure 5-5, Figure 5-6 and Figure 5-7 show some of the more unique arborglyphs from Alabama.

Figure 5-8 shows an arborglyph found in Georgia. It is named the *Turtle man* because of its odd shaped head and rounded body with four legs.

Figure 5-6 Snake Arborglyph

Figure 5-7 Birdman Arborglyph

Figure 5-8 Arborglyph Named The Turtle Man

Figure 5-9 Arborglyph on Beech Tree

Figure 5-10 Arborglyph

Several other example arborglyphs found in the southeast-ern United States are shown in Figures 5-9 and 5-10. These ar-borglyphs were found in north central Alabama.

WITNESS TREES OF FORSYTH COUNTY GEORGIA

The Etowah River in northern Forsyth County dips to the south and then back north forming what appears to be an eagles head. Near this location, the Old Federal Road cross-es over the river heading northwest. The road was authorized by the Cherokees to be built across their nation from west of Augusta, Georgia, to Chattanooga, Tennessee, in 1805. This area was known as Hightower, the English equivalent to the Cherokee word *Etowah*, and it was the home of the Red Bank Cherokees under Chief Rising Fawn's leadership.

The Cherokees knew the State of Georgia and the United States governments were going to remove them to Oklahoma in 1838, and so they set about making preparations long be-fore the day arrived. In the area where the Red Bank Chero-kees lived were several gold and silver mines. The Cherokees mined these claims for years until the State of Georgia made it unlawful for the Cherokees to continue mining. The Red Bank Cherokees knew that if they tried to take their gold and silver possessions with them on the Trail of Tears it would be stolen by the soldiers. Therefore, they made preparations to bury their gold and silver before they left, marking the spots. Forest Wade in his book, *Cry of the Eagle*,[60] stated that the val-ue of the gold of the Red Bank Cherokees at thirty-five dollars per ounce was over $240,000 in 1838.

To mark where they planned to bury their gold, the Chero-kees bent trees and carved arborglyph mysterious map symbols to help them relocate the gold if they could return to Geor-gia. On the night before they were taken from their homes in 1838, the Red Bank Cherokees buried their gold.

Forest Wade, a part Cherokee, learned to read the sym-bols on the trees from a full-blood Cherokee and documented many of the beech trees with the symbols. He shows ten trees in his book but there were many others as documented by other old timers in the county. After writing his book, Forest Wade's daughter, Peggy Dorsey, told of Cherokee descendents returning to Georgia to meet with her father who took them to places to recover their treasure. In his book, Forest Wade drew many of the symbols he found on the trees, but because of the need for secrecy, no meanings were provided. The Cherokees also created pictographs on rocks as part of their maps for their buried treasure.

OTHER TRIBAL ARBORGLYPHS

Archeologist A. T. Jackson studied Indian rock art and pictographs in Texas and published an extensive record of his findings titled *Picture-Writing of Texas Indians.*[61] In his book published in 1938, he recorded the existence of some specially painted trees he located in central Texas that he attributed to the Comanches. The trees had painted or carved designs and are believed to date to the 1830s. These trees were mostly located near the Comanche Trails and were painted in blue and red colors. The painted trees had been found in Edwards, Palo Pinto, San Saba and Wood Counties. Unfortunately, the settlers cut these trees down because they wanted to get rid of Indian markings.

In addition to the painted trees, some trees found in Wood County also had carved designs that include circles, turtles, snakes, and zigzag lines. Interesting about the colors chosen by the Comanche to paint the trees is that the Comanche Nation flag of today has blue and red as its primary colors.

The Indian tribes of the north central and Northeastern United States also painted trees. Schoolcraft reported Cadwallader Colden's account from his book, *History of the Five Nations of Canada*, published in 1747 in London. Quoting Colden, Schoolcraft said,

> *"The general custom prevalent among the Mohawks going to war, was to paint the trunk of a tree with red paint as a symbol of their expedition's purpose. On their return trip, they would visit the same tree and add more symbols to denote their results.*[52]"

Figure 5-11 Northeastern Arborglyph

Schoolcraft also reported again from Colden that when a French Army marched against the Iroquois in 1696, the Iroquois craved a symbol of the French Army on a tree and then piled two bundles of cut rushes numbering 1,434 pieces at the base of the tree to inform the French that the Iroquois would bring that many warriors to fight the French.

Some of the northeastern tribes such as the Iroquois probably also carved arborglyph messages on birch trees. Figure 5-11 shows an arborglyph from a northeastern tribe.

WHITE MAN ADOPTS INDIAN USE of WITNESS TREES

One only has to adventure into the forested areas of our country to find white man's graffiti on trees, rocks and walls of structures. Carving one's initials with a date has long been a standard practice of the masses. Unfortunately, some people also desecrate some of our priceless treasures with their graffiti.

One of the early noted uses of trees with arborglyphs from the settlers is *bearing trees*. In 1812 as more territories were becoming states, the United States began surveying these lands to document their boundaries, roads, trails, rivers and to divide the land for recording the sale to the new settlers. The United States government formed the Government Land Office (GLO) which later became the Bureau of Land Management. Their survey system was the Public Land Survey System which diced the land into square sections known as range and townships all based on a common starting point located in Glasgow, Pennsylvania.

To mark the corners of plats, the surveys used monuments such as a rock pile, a wooden post, or a combination of the two. Trees were also sometimes used when available. These witness trees and the markings made on them, are recorded in the surveyor's official field notes. Witness trees are commonly referred to as bearing trees, and they provide a record of the survey for all subsequent transaction involving that land. Figure 5-12 shows a bearing tree located in Alabama from an 1817 survey. The tree still exited in 2008, and is recorded on the plat document. The tree is a beech tree.

Others learned the practice of using beech trees to write on but not all were for public use. Warren Getler and Bob Brewer wrote *Rebel Gold* and published it in 2003.[62] This story is about the confederate sympathizers who wanted to bring the south back after the Civil War. They formed a group called the Knights of the Golden Circle and set about robbing the Union forces, banks, trains and other sources to gather sufficient money and weapons to stage a comeback. One of their chief robbers was Jesse James.

The Knights of the Golden Circle had an extensive organization made up of a large number of leading citizens across the south and they had a group of men who collected the money and weapons from the robberies and buried them for later use. The burial of this treasure closely followed Chief Rising

Figure 5-12 Bearing Tree in Alabama

Fawn's story from Forest Wade's book. Stand Watie, the Cherokee Chief who was very rebellious in the Cherokee Nation after their removal to Oklahoma, was a major leader in the Knight of the Golden Circle (KGC). He, in fact, was the last Confederate general to surrender on June 23, 1865. Throughout his time in the Confederate forces, he led many guerrilla warfare attacks. It is believed that Stand Watie may have been the person who taught the rest of the KGC how to bend and carve maps on trees to mark where their treasure was buried and for later retrieval. Also, some of the KGC members married Cherokee women who may have also taught how to mark sites. The *Rebel Gold* contains several example arborglyph trees with their carved symbols that are very similar to those found on Cherokee trees.

Chapter 6

BENT TREES OF THE WESTERN TRIBES

The early chapters of this book primarily focused on the bent trees of the eastern Indian tribes. In this chapter and Chapter 7 we will turn our attention to the tribes of the midwest and western states. They also bent and modified trees for various purposes, some different from their eastern brethren.

Figure 6-1 North American Vegetation Coverage 1906

The United States east of longitude W 094.5 degrees is mostly deciduous forests where the Indians easily found hardwood trees to bend for marking trails, water sources, shelter, and more. West of longitude 94.5 degrees, the country changes to grasslands, deserts and a drier climate. Figure 6-1 shows the North American Vegetation Map from 1906. In the Midwest and western states, there are fewer trees to bend or modify and where trees could be found, they were different from those used in the east. The species of trees used by the Indians in the west were mostly pecan, cottonwood and ponderosa pine.

There is a scarcity of documentation on western tribes whose culture included bending trees. Two tribes are known to have used trees similar to the eastern tribes. They were the Comanche and the Ute. The Kiowa, Apache and Cheyenne, who also wandered the west, may have bent trees also.

COMANCHE TREES

Barbara Goodin, an elder of the Comanche Nation, said,

> *"The Comanche's were rulers of the Great Plains in the 1700s and became known as the Lords of the Southern Plains. Renowned for their horsemanship, they defended their land from all intruders. Introduction of the horse to Comanche people enabled them to travel widely, striking terror into the hearts of their farthest enemy. It also enabled them to provide the things necessary for their families -- food, shelter and clothing.[63]"*

The Comanches were not a single tribe but rather many bands, some say as many as thirty-five, headed by a chief. They were nomadic buffalo hunters traveling the plains in search of the herds that provided food, clothing and other essentials to their daily way of life. In following the buffalo herds, they traveled great distances and were constantly in search of places to settle down periodically at a good camp site. Jeff Meyer said,

> *"A good campsite had to be near running water (as a source of water and fish), had to have tall bluffs or hills on at least three sides for lookouts, and very often had a pecan grove. Not only were pecans widely used for food and dye, a grove often signaled good soil for other fruits and berries and abundant wildlife to eat.[64]"*

When a good campsite was found, the Comanches marked it with a bent tree to tell others that might follow behind them that this site was good. At the site, they would find a pecan (or cottonwood) tree that was generally less than ten feet tall and bend it to the ground from its top forming a moon-shaped or rainbow bend in the tree. The tree would usually take a year to become permanently bent into its new shape. The tree thus became a *marker tree*, marking the campground for generations to come. The tree would continue to grow horizontally along the ground and then send a vertical member skyward to reach for the sun.

Some Comanches call these marker trees *turning trees*. Anna Jean Taylor from the Panhandle-Plains Historical Museum in Canyon, Texas, did research on the turning trees in 1996.[65] In her research she worked with Melvin Kerchee, Sr., a Comanche elder, who told her that he learned about the turning trees from his grandfather and other elders who spoke about the trees that were used to mark campsites before the Comanches were moved to a reservation in 1875. With Mr. Kerchee's help and through her own research, Taylor determined the probable location of other campsites used by the Comanches but few of them have the bent trees remaining today.

Linda Pelon began researching the Comanches as part of her masters research at the University of Texas at Arlington in 1993. Pelon's research focused on the Great Trinity Forest area of Dallas, Texas, with which she thought the Comanches had been associated. Pelon's research led to the discovery of a pecan marker tree at the Gateway Park in Dallas. This pecan tree shown in Figure 6-2 was determined to be 290 years old when it died in 1997 due to damage from a storm. Elders from the Comanche Nation visited the site of the Gateway Park Marker Tree in 1997, and proclaimed the tree as a "living monument to our historic presence in Texas."[66]

Figure 6-2 Comanche Marker Tree, Dallas, Texas

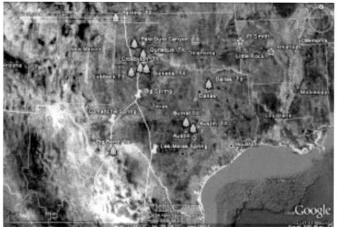

Figure 6-3 Probable Comanche Campsites (green) along Comanche
Trails in Yellow. Water Sites are Yellow Push Pins

Figure 6-3 shows some of the other possible Comanche campsites that were thought to be associated with the Comanche Trail shown in yellow. Turning trees have been found at the Dallas, and Burnet, Texas sites. There is also a tree at Big Bend National Park that is believed to be a Turning Tree but confirmation has not been made by the Comanche. These campsites were delineated in Anna Taylor's research[65] as reported by Comanche elders, archaeologists, historians, and early settlers to the Texas area. The determination of the sites shown in the graphic is based on the normal characteristics expected at a campsite which was a good water source, shelter and high bluffs for lookouts to warn of enemies approaching the camp. Recently, more Comanche trees have been found in Plano, TX.

All of the campsites along the Comanche Trail shown in the Google Earth image have good water sources. Three of the sites, however, have some of the largest springs in Texas. These sites are Big Spring, Comanche Spring, and Las Moras Spring. Comanche Spring was the largest of the three springs pumping over forty-three million gallons per day whereas Las Moras pumps twelve to fourteen million gallons per day. Since the Comanche have left these areas, over pumping of water from the aquifer has impacted the water supply in these springs. Due to the heavy pumping, Comanche Spring dried up in March 1961.

Figure 6-4 Possible Turning Tree, Burnet, TexasY

The Turning Trees at Burnet, Texas and Big Bend National Park are shown in Figures 6-4 and 6-5.

While the Comanche are more noted for the turning trees, they also bent and modified trees for other purposes. Taylor stated in her research that Dr. Dan Gelo, Professor of Anthropology at the University of Texas at San Antonio, had reported that,

"Comanches had also tied down saplings to point to watering holes off the main trail. Some of these trees continued to grow horizontally and served as landmarks."[65]

Figure 6-5 Possible Turning Tree, Big Bend Natioanl Park, Texas

This is very similar to what the eastern tribes did. One last example of trees modified by the Comanche's was reported by Taylor from archaeologist Joe Hayes, Curator, Museum of the Great Plains in Lawton, Oklahoma. One member whose family had settled in the Lubbock, Texas area reported to Hays that,

"their family knew of a place where the Comanche has dug up twelve saplings, split and inserted stones in to each, and planted them around a good spring."[65]

The trees were dwarfed from the insertion of the stone so that they did not cover the spring. This site is believed to be along the Comanche Trail.

The Comanche also decorated some trees with color or carved shapes whose meanings are unknown. Archaeologist A.T. Jackson wrote an extensive book on the picture-writing of the Texas Indians[61] wherein he discussed and showed examples of trees along parts of the Comanche Trail in Edwards, Palo Pinta, San Saba and Wood counties. Some of the trees were painted with red and blue paint on oaks and other trees with smooth skins. Other trees had carved shapes similar to what has been found in the southeast.

While the Comanche were the predominant tribe in Texas, other tribes including the Cherokees, Caddos, and Tonkawas also occupied parts of Texas near the Dallas area. The Dallas Archaeological Society reported in *The Record* in 1941, that some of its members had located Indian trail trees in an area two and one half miles west of Cedar Hill, Texas. They found several trees in that location, now buried under a lake, that were near an old Indian village campsite, believed to have been a Cherokee village based on records of battles with the Cherokees in that area. These trees were post oaks and were located

along the creek area. The Dallas Archaeological Society also reported finding five other marker trees within one half mile of the Irving Trail. Three of these marker trees were in alignment spaced fifteen feet apart and point-

Figure 6-6 Cherokee Trail Trees Near Irving, Texas, 1941

ing in the same direction. The drawing of three of the trees shown in Figure 6-6 was drawn from a photograph taken of the trees.

COMANCHE STORYTELLING SITES

As mentioned previously, a good campsite needed a good water supply and high bluff. Many of the sites delineated in Taylor's research had those characteristics. The high bluff provided a means of protection to the Comanche tribe. It also provided a place for spiritual reflection and for storytelling.

The passing down to the next generation of their tribal history and stories was done orally by the elders. For a tribe that wanders the Great Plains, it is not easy to find one place to gather their younger generations at some commonly used place to tell the stories and to worship their Great Spirit. Therefore, each campsite they visited needed a place to gather and, in the high bluffs above the campsite, they could not only tell their stories but also could be closer to the Great Spirit. People sometimes prayed alone, while other times there were group gatherings.

In the Great Trinity Forest in Dallas, near the campsite of the Turning Tree, there is a special place in the high limestone bluffs above the Trinity River. This place has become known as the Storytelling Place and it is a place sacred to the Comanches. There is an amphitheater quality to it making it an excellent place for the Comanches to tell their stories and to pray to their Great Spirit. Elders from the Comanche Nation visited the Storytelling Place in 2002, and determined the site to have been part of their culture and a place where their oral traditions could take place.[66]

Linda Pelon has worked diligently to preserve this storytelling site from planned developments in the forest. This site is one of the few left associated with the Comanche campsites that remain today.

THE END OF AN ERA

The white man entered the Great Plains in the early 1800s and soon began killing the buffalo in order to sell their hides. The Indians only killed what they needed to survive. The white man killed for economic gain. Before the white man came to the plains, the anthropologists believe there were at least thirty million buffalo there. By 1880, they were almost gone.

The policy of the American Government was to place the Indians on reservations and open the territory to settlers who wanted to raise cattle and farm the vast territory of the Great Plains. The Cattle Barons had many political friends in Washington and a duel policy developed: move the Native People into reservations away from valuable land and destroy the herds of buffalo. Hunters were encouraged to hunt on the Plains to destroy the buffalo.

The killing was vast and relentless. By 1885, the government estimated that only 200 buffalo were alive in the wild. In forty-five years (1840 to 1885) the huge herds had been destroyed with the numbers declining from millions to almostt nothing. With the decrease in the buffalo, a concomitant decrease in the Plains Indians occurred dropping their population by over fifty percent due to loss of food.

General Sheridan of the American Army said,

> *"These men (the buffalo hunters) have done more in two years, and will do more in the next two years, to settle the vexed Indian question, than the entire regular army has done in thirty years...let them kill, skin and sell until the buffaloes are exterminated...then your prairies can be covered with speckled cattle.*[67]*"*

By 1880, both the buffalo and a way of life for the Comanches were gone and they were forced to move to a reservation in Oklahoma. With that move, their nomadic way of life had disappeared and the campsites with turning trees were no longer needed. Unfortunately, many of the marker trees were also known to the settlers who cut them down not wanting anything left related to the Indian culture.

UTE TREES

West of the Great Plains, the Rocky Mountain region begins with its high mountain peaks, high plateaus, deep canyons and alpine forests. The high plateau area west of Colorado Springs centered on Florissant, Colorado, was the territory of the Ute Indians. The Ute Indians were nomadic and forest-dwelling tribes who lived in Colorado, parts of Utah and northern New Mexico. The Spanish introduced the Utes to horses which allowed them to be a more nomadic tribe covering large sections of Colorado and New Mexico in their travels.

Ute land included hunting grounds, along with places of spiritual importance. Pikes Peak was one of the most important spiritual places to the Utes. Some of the tribal members made a spiritual journey there every year.

Ute Marker Trees

Marker trees are all ponderosa pines as are the prayer trees.

Figure 6-7 Ute Marker Tree

This species has a longevity of about 600 years so they will outlast generations of tribal existence. The bending of the ponderosa pine had to be done similarly to the eastern pine species which involved relieving the stress of the outer fibers to keep the tree from breaking in the hip area. The Ute marker trees have similar hip scars that show the tree probably had some material removed to allow the bend of ninety degrees to occur. Figure 6-7 shows a Ute marker tree at Mueller State Park in Colorado. This tree is probably located on the pathway to Pikes Peak since it points directly to the mountain. In the figure you can see the scar on the hip and horizontal section of the tree.

A number of these marker trees have been found in the area once occupied by the Utes. Twenty-five of them exist on Florissant Fossil Beds National Monument land. One rather unique marker tree has been found at the National Monument which is bent all the way to the ground and has three vertical members. A Ute elder told Toby Wells, who was raised on a farm in that area, that,

> "the tree marked the location of a spring and was on a trail used by the Ute."[68]

Toby and his family used the spring as their water supply. Also near the location of the tree was a chipping site for making arrowheads. The unique marker tree is shown in Figure 6-8 with Toby Wells sitting on it.

Figure 6-8 Unique Ute Marker Tree

Prayer Trees

The prayer trees had a special role for the Ute people in their vision quests. Celinda Reynolds Kaelin has spent a number of years working with the Ute elders to learn their customs and to support their yearly return to their homelands in the Florissant Colorado plateau and Pikes Peak area. Through her extensive research, the history and purpose of the prayer trees has been uncovered as told to her by the Utes. She detailed that information in her book *Pikes Peak Backcountry*,[69] and it is repeated with her permission:

> *Mountaintops are thought to have strong spiritual powers among indigenous peoples, including the Utes. Modern scientists have documented highly unusual electromagnetic phenomena on these high peaks, lending further credibility to these traditional teachings. According to Ute elders, one of their principal ceremonies is the 'Vision Quest,' undertaken by an individual on a mountain peak for several days in seclusion and while fasting. During this quest, it is thought that the individual will be given spiritual guidance from the Great Spirit through visions. Pikes Peak was a special focal point for the Ute's Ceremonial Circle, an organization of holy people. This group made periodic journeys to nearby Crystal Peak where they collected stones thought to be imbued with spiritual properties. They then began a pilgrimage to Pikes Peak, following the trail along the mountain ridge, where they finally encamped in the area of the Pancake Rocks. Prayer Trees -- pine saplings that were bent over and tied with a leather thong -- still provide silent testimony to the prayers offered during the course of this pilgrimage along Cedar Mountain road. One individual was then chosen to take all of the spirit stones to the summit of the Peak on a four-day Vision Quest.*[69]

Figure 6-9 shows a typical prayer tree that has been bent low to the ground by the Utes as part of the vision quest culture. One of the more unique prayer trees located in Colorado by Celinda Kaelin is shown in Figure 6-10. This tree is called the Holy Woman Tree. The tie down marks are easily discernable on this tree. Loya Arum, a Ute elder, explained the purpose of the Prayer Tree during an interview in 2008.[21] Standing by the tree shown in Figure 6-10, Loya said,

"We call this tree the Holy Woman Tree. What they would do is bend the tree by tying it down. This would be the altar (main part of the tree). Speaking to the tree, we say we are going to offer tobacco and the offering/prayer ultimately goes to Creator. Then you speak to the ancestors. What I want to say to the ancestors is that we care and love them because we know they are around and I'm here to be with their spirits and the spirit of the tree. The Prayer Tree holds the prayers and then they go to Creator.[21]"

Near the site of the Holy Woman Tree is another unique tree found by Celinda Kaelin which was actually three trees most likely planted together by the Utes and over a time period woven into a braided tree that obviously had a special purpose or meaning.

Figure 6-9 Ute Prayer Tree

Ute Burial Trees

The cedar tree is very important to most Indian tribes as pointed out earlier in this book. To many tribes, the cedar tree has spiritual powers. The cedar tree has also very important to the Utes. The Ute medicine people carried the seeds of the cedar and when another medicine person or a chief died, these seeds were plant-

Figure 6-10 Holy Woman Prayer Tree

ed nearby. These trees are found throughout the Ute territory in Colorado.[70]

This practice is similar to the Ho-Chunk Indians who bent trees to mark the graves of those that died. In all probability, the bent trees marked the grave sites of the more important tribal members who had died along their nomadic paths.

Other Ute Trees

Two other important trees related to the Ute's are the culturally scared tree which is most often called an arborglyph tree and the culturally modified trees (CMT) or more often called a medicine or peeled tree. The Ute arborglyph trees are discussed in Chapter 5, witness trees and the medicine/peeled trees are discussed in Chapter 7.

OTHER WESTERN TRIBE TREES

Other than for the culturally modified trees, there is little evidence that the culture of other western tribes included bending trees. Less than fifty bent ponderosa pines have been located in Colorado, southern New Mexico and northern California. Other bent trees have been reported as being found in northern Arizona. The Apache Indians occupied southern New Mexico and parts of Arizona. They were closely associated with the Comanche so perhaps they followed similar practices.

Chapter 7

CULTURALLY MODIFIED TREES

Culturally modified trees (CMT), also called scarred trees, medicine trees, or peeled trees, have been found worldwide. These trees have been located in the northern hemisphere in Sweden, Turkey, Canada and the United States. In the southern hemisphere, they have been found in Australia and may also exist in New Zealand. In the United States, these trees are mostly associated with the Western tribes and particularly with the tribes of the mountains and northwestern areas of the US. However, they have also been found in the northeast connected with the Iroquois and other eastern tribes. Ponderosa pine is the predominate specie of tree used by the Indians, but cedar, spruce, hemlock, black cottonwood and red alder have also been found with some of the same scarred characteristics found in ponderosa pine.

Culturally modified tree has become the common term used to describe the modification of trees by indigenous people as part of their culture. For the most part, the trees were used by the indigenous people to provide the needs of their lifestyle including food, canoes, cradleboards, medicine, and fiber for making clothing, hats, ropes and blankets. Some examples do exist where the trees were also carved with an arborglyph or sometimes called dendroglyph. Like the bent trees, the CMT have been somewhat hidden from public notice or pursued by researchers until the 1980s. But that has changed greatly; many of the trees are now being preserved in national parks and on Indian lands. These trees are often now called *Living Artifacts.*

Before discussing the CMTs of the United States, we will touch on the related CMTs of other countries.

SCANDINAVIA

The Sami
are an indig-
enous peo-
ple of the
Scandina-
vian part
of north-
ern Europe.
Traditional-
ly, the Sami
were a no-
madic group

Figure 7-1 Sami People in 1900

of people traveling the northern part of Scandinavia herding
reindeer, fishing, and sheep herding. As seen in Figure 7-1,
their lifestyle was not much different from the American Indians of the west.

One of the most informative studies done on the Swed-
ish CMTs was published in 2003 by T.S. Ericsson, Lars Ostlund and Rikard Andersson, *Destroying a Path to the Past – the
Loss of Culturally Scarred Trees and a Change in Forest Structure
along Allmunvagen, in Mid-West Boreal Sweden.*[71] Their study
analyzed a part of an old bridle trail in boreal Sweden where
many scarred trees have been located. The trail was a path to
remote villages in the Fennoscandian Mountains. Parts of that
trail are still visible today.

Their study located a total 104 scarred trees. Using dendrochronology, the date when the tree was culturally modified or
scarred was determined. The oldest trees found (downed) had
an average date of 1765; the old trees (standing) had an average date of 1847; and the youngest trees had an average date
of 1911. Using historical maps and forest surveys from 1876
to 2000, the researchers were able to show that by conserva-
tive estimate ninety percent of the original blazed trees have
vanished due to forest logging and other causes. The authors
stated,

"The trail was interpreted as have being lined for centuries with scarred trees which gradually have been destroyed during the 20th century. Culturally modified trees constitute a unique source of information for understanding pattern of old trails as well as of past human land use and movement in the landscape prior to the 20th century. This biological archive has to a large extent been destroyed by forestry activities, and it is therefore very important to survey, recount and protect the trees that are still present.[71]*"*

The Sami peoples probably harvested the cambium layer of the trees for food value. This layer contained carbohydrates, dietary fiber, vitamin C, and other minerals. These were most likely harvested in the winter months when supplemental sources of food were needed.

CANADA

Knowledge about the culturally modified trees of Canada like the other countries had been limited to a few until the 1980s when it exploded into the news. The Haida Gwaii Nation who occupies the Queen Charlotte Islands in British Columbia began defending their cultural heritage by stopping logging of the old growth spruce, hemlock and cedar timbers that are a principal part of their way of life. The western red cedar has significant cultural value to the Haida. It is used for making canoes, longhouses, hunting and cooking instruments, clothing, totem poles, mortuary poles, masks, rattles and other ceremonial items. The Haida people have for centuries culturally modified the trees of their lands to support their way of life and continue today with those same practices.

Unlike their Indian brethren in the United States, the Haida people have not been removed from their homelands but they have suffered just the same. A smallpox epidemic killed ninety percent of the Haida population in 1850 and if that was not enough to destroy an Indian culture, the British began logging their territory in the 1940s causing untold environmental and cultural damages. Clear-cutting over the last hundred years has not only severely impacted these people's way of life, it has also destroyed many of the culturally modified trees.

In 1985-86, the Haida people had enough and began blocking the logging trucks and the destruction of their forests. Many changes have taken place in the past twenty-five years to protect these forests from destruction but a constant battle continues in order to preserve the Haida cultural heritage.

To help in the identification and preservation of the culturally modified trees in British Columbia, Canada commissioned a report, *Culturally Modified Trees of British Columbia, A Handbook for the Identification Recording of Culturally Modified Trees* pub-

Figure 7-2 British Columbia CMT

COURTESY BC FORESTRY SERVICE

lished in 2001.[72] Today through the efforts of many archaeologists and other researchers, the trees are being saved across Canada wherever they are being found.

The Haida Qwaii Indian tribe is not the only tribe in Canada impacted by the loss of culture due to deforestation. Many others have experienced similar situations and are working with the government to identify and preserve part of their legacy left by their ancestors. Figure 7-2 shows a typical culturally modified tree in the British Columbia province. Hundreds or maybe even thousands of these trees can be found throughout the Canadian provinces today even though many have been lost to logging and other development activities.

Many of these trees are being located and cataloged to preserve them from future logging efforts.

TURKEY

Very little has been written about the culturally modified trees of Turkey. Fortunately, a recent journal report was published in the *Journal of Ethnobiology Fall/Winter 2009* by Nancy J. Turner, Yilmaz Ari, Fikret Berkes, Iain Davidson-Hunt, Z. Fusun Ertug and Andrew Miller. Their journal paper, "*Cultural Management of Living Trees: An International Perspective,*"[73] provided some insights into the Turkish use of pines for food.

Some of the culturally modified trees in Turkey were found near the ruins of the Roman city of Lydae which is near the current city of Gocek, Turkey. The Turkish people used Turkish pine (Pinus brutia) and Scots pine (Pinus sylvestris) to harvest the cambium layer which they called *Yalabuk* as a food source delicacy. The authors of the journal article reported on one referenced source documenting the Turkish use of trees. The referenced source is Yasar Kemal, a leading Turkish author, who interviewed villagers in the Taurus Mountains east of Antalya, Turkey in the 1950s. Kemal observed heavy modifications in most of the pine trees due to the consumption of inner bark (yalabuk). In addition to its good taste, people attested healing power to the yalabuk, particularly for tuberculosis.[73]

AUSTRALIA

The Aboriginal people of the Australian Provinces (States) in Queensland, New South Wales and Victoria culturally modified trees as part of their traditional culture. There is also

Figure 7-3 Scarred Aboriginal Tree Preserved in Fitzroy Gardens, Australia

a report of some trees being modified near Perth, Australia, in the Western Province. Aboriginal people removed bark from trees to make canoes, containers and shields and to build temporary shelters. Many of the scarred trees that have been located in Australia are over 200 years old. The largest number of the trees is located in Lake Boort Reserve northwest of Melbourne. This site has 900 red gums and black box trees scarred by the Dja Dja Wurrung people. However, the site may be lost to development unless the Australian government saves it.

The most common native trees used by the aboriginal people are the species river red Gum (Eucalyptus camaldulensis) and yellow box (Eucalyptus melliodora) which occurs along the majority of inland waterways and creek lines.

Figure 7-3 shows a typical Aboriginal scarred tree found in Australia. This one is located in the Fitzroy Gardens, State of Victoria, Australia. The tree, although dead, has been preserved. The plague on the tree reads:

> *"The scar on this tree was created when Aboriginal people removed bark to make canoes, shields, food and water containers, string, baby carriers and other items. Please respect this site. It is important to the Wurundjeri people as traditional custodians of the land and is part of the heritage of all Australians."*

The Australian government, like the Canadian government has been pro-active in preservation efforts for the scarred or culturally modified trees of the Aboriginal peoples. Most of these trees are the typical scarred tree as shown in Figure 7-3. However, it has been reported that the Aboriginal people also created trees that are called boundary trees and possibly arborglyph trees.

Some Aborigines told a researcher about how the boundary trees were created. They said,

> *"Boundary trees were created by tying gum tree branches (or in the case of very young trees, entire trunks) together with kangaroo sinews. With time the branches or trunks would knit together to form a very distinctive shape. Such trees signified the boundaries between various tribes and clans. Sometimes they were also marked by carving various symbols into the bark.[74]"*

Boundary trees and scarred trees formed a system of signage throughout the Australian landscape. Aborigines would read the trees just as we read street signs and traffic lights. Unfortunately, European settlers cut down many of these trees and so there are now big gaps in the system. On forming the boundary tree, the Aborigines bent the limbs/trunks together to form a circle in the tree. Figure 7-4 is a boundary tree that remains today. The circle has almost closed up but it is still visible.

Figure 7-4 Aboriginal Boundary Tree

Figure 7-5 Aboriginal Australian Arborglyph Carving

The arborglyphs, also called dendroglyphs, of the Aboriginal peoples of Australia began to be recorded in 1817 by government surveys. The majority of these were found in New South Wales Province. At one site in New South Wales, the surveyors discovered a tumulus grave consisting of a large oblong mound with three semi-circular seats. Overhanging the grave were several cypress trees that were fancifully carved.[75] Figure 7-5 shows some of the type carvings found on the Aboriginal arborglyph trees. Several detailed studies were done of these carvings and they are housed in the Australian Museums. The Australian Aboriginal carvings are some of the most intricate and skilled carvings among all the indigenous peoples worldwide.

THE CULTURALLY MODIFIED TREES OF THE NATIVE AMERICAN INDIANS

The culturally modified trees (CMT) found in the United States are mostly located in the northwestern region of the country and in Alaska. Many of the CMT trees used by the Indians are of the ponderosa pine (Pinus ponderosa) species. However, research by Leslie M. Johnson Gottesfeld from the University of Alberta, Canada in 1992 detected twenty-one species which played a certain role as CMTs. This research covered the area of Canada and the United States. The tree species identified by Gottesfeld that were most often used were:

> "the Western Red Cedar (Thuja plicata), Yellow Cedar (Chamaecyparis nootkatensis), spruces (Picea glauca), Hemlock (Tsuga heterophylla), pines (Pinus

contorta, Pinus ponderosa). In addition, Quaking Aspen (Populus tremuloides), Black Cottowood also know as Western Balsam Poplar (Populus tricho-carpa) and Red Alder (Alnus rubra) are also quite frequently found. The bark of hemlock and certain spruces was important for nourishment and medi-cine. The resin of spruces was used as a kind of glue.[76"]

Thirty to forty years ago, before the Canadian Indians began protesting the loss of their cultural heritage in the clear-cutting of their forests, little was known about the CMTs. Now today in the United States, CMT is becoming more of a commonly heard term and researchers, foresters and preservationists are busily documenting these historical living treasures.

By 1985, a protection program was started in the Gifford Pinchot National Forest in the State of Washington. More than 6,000 CMTs were identified in the forest and many of them are now protected. More have been found in the Ashley National Forest located in northeastern Utah and Wyoming, a place once occupied by the Utes. In Montana, about 200 CMTs were located at the Bob Marshall Wilderness and others have been found in the Glacier National Park. The trees found in Montana are believed to have been modified by the Salish and Kootenai tribes of that area.

Colorado was the homelands of the Utes and there many CMTs have also been found. Seventeen CMTs were found in the Blue Mountain area within Pike National Forest, another twenty-six found in Florissant Fossil Beds National Monument and others were found in the Manitou Experiment Forest near Woodland Park. Eleven Mile and Mueller State Parks and the area surrounding Florissant, Colorado also contain many. Also in Colorado at the Great Sand Dunes National Park, over one hundred of the CMTs have been located. In February 2008, the Colorado Historical Society decided to invest a part of its budget into a project to document the CMTs at the Mesa Verde National Park located in the southwest corner of Colorado. This was the home of the ancient Pueblo people known as the Anasazi.

In the far northern State of Alaska, in its southeastern region, CMTs also have been found at Bartlett Bay, Glacier National Park and on Ship Island north of Ketchikan, Alaska.

THE EVIDENCE OF THE CMT's EXISTENCE IS VALIDATED

There is no longer a doubt about how the CMTs were created and who did it. Over the past thirty years, the Indians and
indigenous people worldwide have confirmed that their ancestors peeled and scarred the trees. Today, in some areas, the
practice of culturally modifying and using the trees as part of
their lifestyle continues. Elders have been interviewed; prominent archaeologists, anthropologists, ethnobiologists, and other academic researchers have written referred journal papers
and completed PhD dissertations on the subject of the CMTs.
Even forest rangers from national and state parks and forests
have concluded that the trees are historical and should be preserved as a part of the country's heritage. Further, many of the
studies have cored the trees to age them and the dates of the
tree modifications clearly show they were done at a time that
only the Indians or indigenous peoples occupied those areas.
The evidence is overwhelming and the case is closed. The Living Artifacts are being preserved.

AGING OF THE TREES

Many of the archaeologists, ethnobiologists, and forest
rangers have been coring the CMTs to age the time when they
were scarred. In the Bob Marshall Wilderness in Montana, the
scar on the oldest tree was found to be from 1665 with most of
the tree scars determined to be from the 1851-1875 time period and ending in the 1920-1950 period.[77] In Colorado, archaeologist Marilyn Martorano, who has spent extensive time
researching the CMTs, has recorded a date of 1729 at the Florissant Fossil Beds National Monument with most of the trees
being from the 1815-1875 time period. She has also cored
trees at the Great Sand Dunes National Park and Preserve dated from 1753 to the early 1900s.[78] The trees located at the
Manitou Experimental Forest near Woodland Park, Colora-

do, were recorded as being over 200 years old. In the Ashley National Forest near where the Utes were moved to a reservation in the late 1800s, none of the trees were scarred until after 1900. Lastly, in Alaska, the trees were aged from 1718 to 1912 with most being in the 1852-1895 time period.[79, 80]

The dates of the US trees are consistent with those measured in Canada which are mainly in the 1800s but due to the old growth forests in parts of Canada, some of the dates of the scars date back into the 1700s and one was recorded as 1642.

HARVESTING THE INNER BARK FOR FOOD AND MEDICINE

Turner, Ari, Berkes, Davison-Hunt, Ertuz and Miller said in the paper in the *Journal of Ethnobiology*,

> *"People worldwide have eaten fresh or dried/processed inner bark tissues (phloem, cambium and perhaps some current years of xylem cells) of many tree species. Among different cultures, edible inner bark has been a famine or emergency food, a staple food, a medicinal or health food, and a rare delicacy. The inner bark of many species, at the right stage and weather conditions, is sweet and good-tasting. It contains relatively high concentrations of sugars and vitamin C.*[73]*"*

The Turks described the inner bark, the yalabuk, of their pine trees as a delicacy. The Native American and Canadian tribal elders did also. Two brief articles written by staff members of the Ashley National Forest capture the essence of the value of the inner bark of the CMTs. Keith Stephenson's article, undated, is entitled *"Bark, It's What's for Dinner"* and Byron Loosle's article written in 2003 is called *"So Delicious They Ate the Bark off the Trees."* Marilyn Martorano did an analysis of the value of the cambium layer[78] and Stephenson put it into the nutrition facts format shown in Figure 7-6. Martorano said that one pound of cambium layer was equal to nine glasses of milk.

The Indians used a wooden stick to remove the bark from the tree to get to the cambium layer. Then they used a scraping tool made of a bone or later a can lid to remove the thin

Nutrition Facts

Serving size. 1 lb (464g) of inner bark of Pinus ponderosa

Amount Per Serving

Calories 595   Cal. From Fat 25

	% Daily Value*
Total Fat 2.7g	4%
Ash 8.2g	100%
Sodium 34mg	7%
Total Carbohydrate 138.5g	46%
Dietary Fiber 25g	110%
Sugars 10.8g	25%
Protein 4.5g	

Calcium 2740mg * Sodium 34mg

Magnesium 173mg. * Zinc 9mg

Phosphorus 112mg * Iron 4.5mg

* Percent Daily Values is based on a 2,000 calorie diet. Your daily values may be higher or lower depending on your calorie needs.

Figure 7-6 Cambium Nutritional Facts

white layer from the bark. Once the cambium material was removed, it was usually rolled into balls and wrapped in material to save it for eating later. Sometimes it was cut into small strips and tied together to be eaten.

The bark peeling was usually done in the spring when the sap began to rise again in the tree. In the colder climate of the mountains, this usually occurred in May. However, as pointed out by Martorano in her article *"So Hungry, They Ate the Bark off the Tree,"*[81] the Utes sometimes were starving and resorted to removing the cambium layer of the tree to survive whenever they needed food supplement.

Because of the widespread use of relying on the cambium layer for food over centuries, it's not known where the Indians learned about the food source of the trees. Howev-

Figure 7-7 Ute Ponderosa Pine CMT in Colorado

er, perhaps the Utes watched the animals and in particular the Abert's squirrel. This squirrel relies on the ponderosa pine as a source of food during the entire year. The inner bark, seeds, buds and flowers are all eaten. Marlin Merrill, an interpretive ranger at Eleven Mile State Park in Colorado said,

"The Abert squirrels prefer certain pines (ponderosa); they get up in the trees and cut off the small limbs which drop to the ground. The squirrels then peel the branches to eat the cambium layer which is nutritious to them.[82]*"*

Figure 7-8 CMT in Ashley National Forest, Utah

The exact medicinal value of the cambium layer is unknown. However, the inner layer of the trees used as CMTs has high concentrations of carbohydrates, dietary fiber, vitamin C, and minerals. These were very important in the diet of the indigenous peoples.

Figure 7-7 and Figure 7-8 show typical scarred trees with a section of the cambium layer removed. Figure 7-9 shows a CMT where a large section of the bark was peeled for multiple purposes.

Figure 7-9 CMT Tree in Gifford Pinchot National Forest, Washington

Figure 7-10 Entwined CMT in Colorado

One last type of CMT that is rarely found is the entwined tree. Entwined trees have been intentionally entwined, resulting in their merging into an unusual form. Some of these ponderosa pines have been found along the Canadian and US border. They were entwined by Lakes Salish people moving south when the international boundary was surveyed in 1857, allegedly *to symbolize friendship of the US and Canada.*[83] These may be similar to the boundary trees entwined by the Aboriginal peoples of Australia. At one site in Colorado, an entwined tree was located related to the Ute occupation of that area. This tree is shown in Figure 7-10. Its meaning is unknown.

Chapter 8

TREATY AND COUNCIL TREES

The Indian philosophy of life was simple. All things are living and all things are part of the web of life and deserve respect. The Indian way of life was founded on being close to the earth and all things in human and in nature were important. A quotation attributed to Chief Sitting Bull said,

> *"Every seed is awakened and so is all animal life. It is through this mysterious power that we too have our being and we therefore yield to our animal neighbors the same right as ourselves, to inhabit this land."*

The following quotation is attributed to Haida Indian Chief Skidegate in a tribal council meeting in 1966:

> *"People are like trees, and groups of people are like forests. While the forests are composed of many different kinds of trees, these trees intertwine their roots so strongly that it is impossible for the strongest winds which blow on our Islands to uproot the forest, for each tree strengthens its neighbor, and their roots are inextricably entwined. Just as one tree standing alone would soon be destroyed by the first strong wind which came along, so is it impossible for any person, any family, or any community to stand alone against the troubles of this world."*

The previous chapters in this book clearly show that trees were of great importance to the indigenous peoples and therefore, any major event associated with their life and history would probably involve a place of great significance. Those places often were associated with a special tree. Kerry Holton, Chief of the Delaware (Lenape) Nation said, "Trees were spiritual to the Indians."[1] Thus, when the first treaty to be signed between the colonists and the Indians took place, it was under a special elm tree in what is now Philadelphia, Pennsylvania.

In 1682, The Lenape chiefs signed a treaty with William
Penn under the shade of an American elm along the banks of
the Delaware River. This tree became known as the Shackamaxon Elm. This was the first treaty ever signed by the colonists and it lasted forty years, the longest of any treaty ever
signed by the Colonial or United States government. This treaty allowed the Lenape and William Penn's Quakers to co-exist in the area which later became Pennsylvania. The legend
of William Penn's treaty with the Indians became a universal
symbol of religious and civil liberties and it was documented
in many artist renderings.

Chief Kerry Holton said,

> *"During the Revolutionary War, the British built a*
> *fort next to the Shackamaxon Elm and posted a guard*
> *around the tree because of its importance. If any one*
> *got close to the tree, they would be shot. Then in 1810,*
> *a storm blew it down and everyone came from all*
> *over to see the tree. It was so important, they had to*
> *see the tree."*[1]

The Shackamaxon Tree was the first treaty tree to be so designated in the United States. Today, the site of the Treaty Elm is
known as Penn Treaty Park. A replacement elm tree was planted at the site of the Shackamaxon Elm in 1993, but it did not
survive so another one was planted in the park in 2000. Three
hundred years later, the treaty site still commands great respect
from all peoples. Figure 8-1 shows the William Penn statue in
the park. Today, the Friends of Penn Treaty Park are continuing to show respect for the site of the first treaty in America.
The Lenape Indians are also involved in helping to keep this
place a special place in the history of the United States.

Every treaty signed after the 1682, failed to last as long
as the William Penn – Lenape Treaty, some being broken almost before the ink was dry. Yet even though the Indians were
cheated continuously, they probably considered the subsequent treaty events to be a symbol of entwining their lives with
that of the white man and the event needed to be conducted

Figure 8-1 Penn Treaty Park, Pennsylvannia

at a place of importance. Throughout the Indian-US history, there are many trees that played a role in treaties. Some of those trees still exist as of 2010.

In the historical period of the United States before the mid 1900's, there existed some of the largest specimen trees throughout the country. These trees of various species stood above the surrounding forests and had circumferences in some cases greater than thirty feet. These are the trees that the Indians considered important for council or treaty sites, for trail markers and for places to camp. These trees ranged in age from a mere two hundred years old to over five hundred years. Most of these trees are now gone but a few remain.

SOME OF THE WELL KNOWN TREATY – COUNCIL TREES

There were possibly hundreds of treaty-council tree sites across the United States at some point in our history. Knowledge of these sites was recorded in the literature, but with the loss of the trees and the loss of cultural history for some, they have dropped from existence and have been lost. In the following paragraphs, some of the more important treaty-council trees are discussed briefly.

Some of these trees are remembered only as being used for a treaty signing site; others were used by the Indians as sites for councils and still others were used for both.

Treaty Oak of Austin Texas
(also known as the Council Oaks Site)

This live oak tree estimated to be over 500 years old still stands today in a small park in the city of Austin, Texas. The fact that the tree is still living (2010) is testimony to the hardiness of the tree. In 1989, a resident of Austin tried to poison the tree, yet through the great effort of the city and with the help of many who donated monies, the tree survived.

This is the lone survivor of a grove of fourteen live oak trees that existed at this site. This site was a council site to the Comanche and Tonkawa Indians. The Indians regarded this grove of oaks as being spiritual, almost myth-like and a place of the tree god. They gathered here often to celebrate feasts, to conduct religious ceremonies, to smoke the peace-pipe and on occasion to dance the war dances. This tree is also considered to be the place of a treaty signing between the Father of Texas, Stephen Austin, and the Comanche to establish boundaries between the settlers and the Indians. No documentation has been found to validate the signing of the treaty, but legend says it was the case and hence the tree is called the Treaty Oak.

Treaty Oak of the Treaty of Hopewell, SC

The United States government signed the Hopewell Treaty with the Cherokees in November 1785 and the Choctaws and Chickasaws in January 1786 under an oak tree that was located at the time on the plantation of Andrew Pickens which is near present day Clemson, South Carolina. Less than a mile north of the oak was the then-abandoned Cherokee village site of Essenecca. This treaty established new boundaries between the United States government and the Cherokees after the Revolutionary War wherein the Cherokees gave up a lot of their territory after siding with the British. Territorial boundaries were also established with the Choctaws and Chickasaws.

The Old Treaty Elm of Fort Dearborn, Chicago, ILL.

Under the spreading branches of this magnificent elm tree that stood until 1933, the Indian Treaty of 1835 was signed between Chief Sauganash of the Potawatomi Indians and the United States government. This treaty established boundaries for the Potawatomi reservation near the Fort Dearborn site. The Potawatomi's who had sided with the British during the War of 1812 burned Fort Dearborn to the ground and killed many of its residents. The fort was later rebuilt in 1816 and then abandoned after 1832 when peace with the Indians was established.

Medicine Creek Treaty Tree, Thurston County, Washington

SuAnn Reddick and Cary Collins said in their historical journal report that,

> "This Treaty Tree (douglas fir) stands at the place where on a dreary Christmas Day in 1854 Governor Issac Stevens negotiated terms of the Medicine Creek treaty with some seven hundred Nisqually, Puyallup, Squaxin, Steilacoom and other Indians whose territory embraced four thousand square miles. Here was born the bitter conflict that erupted when the Indians peoples in Washington and Oregon territories confronted the power of the US government as it sought to move the Indians out of the way of the white settlers.[84]"

The site of this treaty was a sacred site to the Indians which they did not want to give up. The treaty, however, moved the Indians to lands that were almost uninhabitable. That led to continual conflicts, some of which continue to today.

The douglas fir tree died in 1979 when the highway department moved a right-a-way that impacted the tree. A winter storm ultimately blew it over leaving just a snag sticking up. *Seattle Times* reporter Lynda Mapes interviewed Indian leader Billy Frank in 2007 at the site of the Treaty Tree. Billy Frank said in that interview with Mapes,

> "What scares the tribes now is our way of life continually, every day is eroded. Puget Sound is dying. Our rivers and cricks have no water. There's not trees, no

huckleberries, no salmon. No hunting and gathering.
No roots, no medicines. Through signing the treaty,
these are supposed to be protected. And they are not.[85"]

Seeds from the treaty tree were collected before it died and
new groves of trees have been planted since 1975. These trees
are growing tall and survive today as a reminder of the Treaty
Tree of Medicine Creek.

1875 Allison Council Tree

In the western states, the oaks and elms give way to the cot-
tonwoods and other western tree species. Near Chadron, Nebraska, stood a lone cottonwood tree known as the Allison
Council Tree. President Grant appointed the Allison Commission in 1875 to negotiate with the Sioux Indians to give up

their rights to the
Black Hills area
of Nebraska. Sen-
ator Allison and
the Sioux Chiefs
and elders met
under the cot-
tonwood tree
for several days
but no treaty or
agreement was
reached. This

Figure 8-2 Creek nation Council Burr Oak Tree

magnificent tree stood sixty feet high and had a circumference
of twenty-two feet. It died in the 1970s.

Creek Nation Council Tree, Tulsa Oklahoma

With the signing into law of the Indian Removal Act of
1830, the migration westward began. The Lochapoka clan
of the Creek Indians began their migration in late 1834 and
finally all arrived by 1836 in present day Tulsa, Oklahoma.
When they left Alabama, they extinguished their council fires
and brought the ashes with them on the long trek. Soon after arriving at their new lands, the elders climbed to the top

of a small hill overlooking the Arkansas River and there under a large Burr oak tree they relit their council fires in a solemn ceremony. The Creek gathered under that tree until late in 1896 for ceremonies, feasts and other council meetings. The Burr oak is today on the National Register and it still stands as shown in Figure 8-2.

Treaty Tree at Chippewanung Creek, Indiana

In 1836, a treaty was signed with the Potawatomi's to give up their lands along Chippewanung Creek in Indiana. The Potawatomi marked the site of the treaty signing with a sycamore tree. The tree was bent like many Indian trees and shaped.

Figure 8-3 Chippewanung Creek Treat Tree

©FULTON COUNTY HISTORICAL SOCIETY, ROCHESTER, IN

Over time the tree grew very large. Shirley Willard and Judy Cecrle of the Fulton County Historical Society said,

> *"This huge sycamore tree was a sapling when the 1836 treaty was signed and the Potawatomi made it grow with a limb parallel to the ground for about twenty feet. The tree trunk is over six feet across with a large limb rising up from its point of beginning ten feet up the trunk. The trunk is now hollow but the tree is still standing in 1978.*[85] *"*

Before the tree died its shape took on the appearance of an eagle shown in Figure 8-3.

The Chippawanung Treaty led to the forced removal of the Potawatomis Indians from the area of Indiana. It became known as the Trail of Death.

One of the most comprehensive studies done on historic trees in the United States was published in 1922 by Katharine Stanley Nicholson in her book *Historic American Trees.*[11] Her work led to the documentation of a number of Indian treaty and council trees throughout the United States. A short sketch of a few of the trees she documented have been extracted from her book digitized by Google and reported here to show further the extent and existence of these type trees.

KATHARINE NICHOLSON HISTORIC AMERICAN TREES

Wi-Ten-A-Ge-Mot Oak

This oak tree was planted by Governor Andros near Schagticoke, New York, probably in 1676 as part of a council meeting between the colonial governor and the Indians. Over 1,000 Indian warriors from the Iroquois, Hoosacs, Pequots, Narragansetts, Pennacooks, Delaware, Mohawks, and other nations were summoned to the council meeting with the governor to establish friendly relationships. In 1922, Nicholson reported the tree to be in its third century of life and twenty-two feet in circumference.[11]

Council Oak of the Santa Fe Trail, Kansas

The US government met with the chiefs of the Osage Indians in the Kansas Territory in 1825 to negotiate a treaty for securing the rights to build the Santa Fe Trail through the Osage Lands. The treaty was signed under a large oak tree. Today, all that remains of that oak is a stump and a plaque.[11]

The Treaty Tree of Indian Springs, GA

The Creek Nation in 1825 was principally two groups, the Upper Creeks living in Alabama and the Lower Creeks living in Georgia. The Lower Creeks were under the leadership of General William McIntosh of Creek lineage. Georgia government officials met with the Upper and Lower Creeks in 1823 to get them to sell their land between the Chattahoochee and Flint Rivers. The Upper Creeks refused but the Lower Creeks decided for the sale and met with the officials at Indian Springs, Georgia, in 1825 under a large poplar tree measuring twelve feet in circumference and signed away their lands. The Upper Creeks were angry about the sale of their lands and killed McIntosh for signing the treaty.[11]

The Elm at Italy Hollow

This tree was located in New York State near the towns of Potter and Middlesex and was known as Big Elm. The tree had a circumference of thirty-two feet. This tree was a favorite Indian council tree as it stood at the junction of several Indian trails where the Indians could come and camp for their council meetings.[11]

The Treaty Tree of Grosse Ile, Michigan

At the time of the signing of the Declaration of Independence, a treaty was signed at Grosse Ile, Michigan, near what is now Detroit between the new United States government and the Indians. They met under the large basswood tree of Grosse, Illinois. Under the treaty Grosse, Illinois, was conveyed to two merchants of Detroit for little money. Representing the Indians were members for the Fox, Sacs, Kikapoos and Potawatomi Indian Tribes. The tree died in 1901, and the site has been commemorated with a stone monument and plaque.[11]

OTHER TREATY – COUNCIL TREES

There are too many other treaty-council trees to mention. However, a few deserve recognition. In Arkansas at the Council Oak Park near the city of Dardanelle, two large 400-500-year-old white oak trees known as the Council Oaks are located. Under these trees in 1820, the then Arkansas Territorial governor met with Chief Black Fox of the Cherokees to negotiate the ceding of the Cherokee lands south of the Arkansas River. This was the beginning of the Cherokees losing all their lands in Arkansas to the massive influx of white settlers into the Arkansas Territory. Later in 1828, the remaining Cherokee territory was given up and the Cherokees moved once again, this time to Oklahoma, their final homelands. Figure 8-4 shows a picture of one of the Council Oaks in Arkansas.

Figure 8-4 Arkansas Council Oak

The Cameron Council Oak was located near Oshkosh, Wisconsin. This 350-year-old Burr oak tree was used by the Indians as a place to hold council meetings when they occupied the area of Wisconsin. The tree was cut down to make way for a University of Wisconsin - Oshkosh campus.[16]

On the bluffs overlooking the Missouri River at Sioux City, Iowa, stood a Burr oak tree that was at least 150 years old when the Lewis and Clark Expedition arrived in early 1800. This tree was used by the Indians for councils for many years and they probably met with Lewis and Clark under the tree. The tree was 350 years old when it died in 1971. A new Burr oak has been planted to replace to Council Tree.

The Neenah Treaty Tree was located at the mouth of the Neenah-Fox River in Wisconsin. This massive elm tree was so large that it was used to guide boatman and steamer pilots on Lake Winnebago. It was a principal place for Indian tribes from Wis-

Figure 8-5 Ute Council Tree

consin to gather for council meetings and for treaty transactions. The tree was lost in 1890 when the river channel had to be widened.[16]

In the far west, the Indians also had trees that were used often for council meetings. The town of Delta Colorado straddles the Ute trail from the Uncompangre Plateau near Olathe, Colorado, to the Grand Mesa in northern Colorado. Near Delta is a cottonwood tree that was a Ute council tree. Figure 8-5 shows the tree.

SPECIAL SITES OF THE INDIGENOUS PEOPLES

Many sites sacred to the Indians are either covered in trees or had at one time large groves of trees. Some of these sites may have been used for councils, but many are places where the tribes gathered for sacred ceremonies and festivities. The United Nations Declaration on the Rights of Indigenous Peoples was adopted by the UN General Assembly on September 13, 2007. This law will become a tool for eliminating human rights violations against the 370 million Indigenous peoples of the world. Article 12 says,

> *"Indigenous peoples have the right to manifest, practice, develop and teach their spiritual and religious traditions, customs and ceremonies and the right to maintain, protect and have access in privacy to their religious and cultural sites."{*

Most of these sacred sites are under constant attack from development with the ultimate destruction of some. The Medicine Lake Highlands near Mt. Shasta, California, sacred to the Wintu, Karuk, Modoc, Shasta and other tribal nations has been used for centuries to train tribal medicine people. The Bureau of Land Management has opened this site to development by energy companies. The San Francisco Peaks in northern Arizona is also sacred to many southwestern Indian tribes. This site is already being used as a ski resort and is being expanded and desecrated. In southern California, the Memorial Oak Grove was important to many tribes from that area. The

University of California decided to clear cut the site and build a sport facility. Indians protested and sat in the trees for 648 days before they were arrested and the site clear cut.

Protection of all Indian sites and artifacts is a must. This is important not only to the Indian but also to all Americans as it is part of our country's heritage.

The ending of this chapter brings us to the close of Living Artifact trees before moving on to Indian trails and artifacts related to the trails. An appropriate way to end this chapter is to quote the poem written in 1913 by Alfred Joyce Kilmer, who single-handedly did more to protect our natural heritage of trees than many others in our past:

> *"I think that I shall never see*
> *A poem lovely as a tree.*
> *A tree whose hungry mouth is prest*
> *Against the earths sweet flowing breast.*
> *A tree that looks at God all day,*
> *And lifts her leafy arms to pray:*
> *A tree that may in summer wear*
> *A nest of robins in her hair.*
> *Upon whose bosom snow has lain;*
> *Who intimately lives with rain.*
> *Poems are made by fools like me,*
> *But only God can make a tree."*
>
> -Alfred Joyce Kilmer

A sad note on the Joyce Kilmer Forest in North Carolina that Kilmer worked so hard to save is that the Hemlock Woolly Adelgid pest devastated the century old hemlocks and eventually killed them in 2009. One hundred and fifty hemlock trees that were the largest in the county had to be removed from the forest in late 2010.

Chapter 9

RELATED INDIAN CULTURAL ARTIFACTS ROCK CAIRNS AND FISH WEIRS

In this chapter we transition from the discussion of the various trees used by the Indians to the Indian trails which begins in Chapter 10. Many of the trail trees are related to trails either to point direction or to mark places of water, shelter or medicinal sites. Now we come to two other artifacts that are also related to the trails and in some cases to the trees.

Some rock cairns and rock structures have been dated as far back as 3000 BCE. The medicine wheel rock structures found in the Midwest and Canada are from that period of indigenous peoples in North American. The rock cairns being discovered today are, for the most part, of a more recent time period but some date into historical indigenous periods. Typically, a rock cairn is a cylindrical stacked-stone structure with a base of about six feet and height of approximately four to six feet. Many of the cairns have more of a conical shape being smaller at the top than at the base. A typical rock cairn is shown in Figure 9-1. Usually they are made of

Figure 9-1 Typical Rock Cairn Structure

flat stones and stacked so as to lean in toward the center of the structure. In some locations where these structures are found, there is no local supply of rock so they have been transported from a great distance to build the structure.

Fish weirs also date to the early indigenous periods. Frederick Johnson did several archaeological digs near Boylston Street in Boston on remnants of a fish weir located there. The fish weir was dated from about 1000 to 3000 BCE.[87] Fish weirs were even mentioned in the *Magna Carta* of 1215 in paragraph 33 which stated,

"All fish-weirs shall be removed from the Thames, the Medway, and throughout the whole of England, except on the sea coast."[88]

ROCK CAIRNS

Based on archaeological and other reported evidence, rock cairns were used for a multitude of purposes. Some are related to marking trails, while others commemorate graves sites and still others for various purposes. *The Nineteenth Annual Report of the Bureau of American Ethnology*, Smithsonian Institute reported in 1898,

"Stones cairns were formally very common along the trails throughout the Cherokee country, but are now almost gone, having been demolished by treasure hunters after the occupation of the country by the whites. They were usually sepulchral monuments built of large stones piled loosely together above a body to a height of sometimes six feet or more, with a corresponding circumference. This method of internment was used only when there was a desire to commemorate the death, and every passer-by was accustomed to adding a stone to the heap. This custom is ancient and world-wide, and still kept up in Mexico and in parts of Europe and Asia.[89]*"*

Another archaeological report on the use of rock cairns for commemorative purposes along trails was published in the *Anthropological Papers of the American Museum of Natural History* related to findings near an Indian village site at Sanger, North Dakota. The report stated,

"Mr. Sanger, a first settler in the vicinity, tells of visiting the village site in company with several Indians of the Fort Berthold Reservation. As they went along, each Indian picked up a small stone and when the party reached the cairn each individual carefully placed his stone on the pile. The Indians told Mr. Sanger that they did this in memory of their ancestors who formerly lived there.[90]*"*

Similar reports of the respect afforded the cairns have been reported in other early writings of observed Indian culture. One report in particular is worthy of note. This report by Thomas Jefferson is included in his *Notes of the State of Virginia* and published in 1853. Jefferson reported activities by one Indian hunting party that happened by his area of Virginia. They left a trail nearby and came to visit a burial site near his home. The burial site in this case was not a cairn but rather a mound of some considerable size. The Indians, in all probability, had traveled a great distance to hunt and knew where to turn off the trail (possibly a marker tree) to locate this burial site some distance from the trail. Jefferson noted,

"But on whatever occasion they may have been made (burial barrow), they are of considerable notoriety among the Indians; for a party passing, about thirty years ago, through the part of the country where this barrow is, went through the woods directly to it, without any instructions or enquiry, and having staid about it some time, with expressions which were construed to be those of sorrow, they returned to the high road, which they had left about a half a dozen miles to pay this visit, and pursued their journey.[91]*"*

Some of the rock cairns found are related to finding or producing water. In the papers on *Archaeology of the Missouri Valley*, George Will reported that,

"In the region west of the Missouri (River) and extending to the Bad Lands, large rock cairns are frequently noticed on the tops of many of the highest hills or buttes. There were probably built by the Dakota, some of whom say that they mark points whence good water can be seen."[90] *"*

David Stuart said in his book, *Anasazi America: Seventeen Centuries on the Road from Center Place* that

"the Anasazi were known for building rock cairns in the desert area with the center of the rock structure left open. The early morning dew would collect on the rocks and when they warmed up the dew would run in the bottom of the structure and was collected for use.[92]*"*

Rock Cairns and Indian Trails

Many of the reference documents cited so far show that there is some relationship in the building of the rock cairns near Indian Trails or using them to mark trails. What is being discovered in Georgia and Arkansas currently is further validating the relationship between the cairns and the trees.

In Georgia, several sites have been found where there are rock cairns near the trails and in some cases co-located with an Indian trail tree. One site has three rock

Figure 9-2 Trail Trees on Old Indian Trail near Rock Cairns

cairns aligned in a straight line equally spaced apart at a bearing of 135 degrees looking out from the top of a mountain.

There is a trail tree at this site as seen in Figure 9-2 marking the trail that is near the center of the picture. The three rock cairns, now destroyed by treasure hunters, are off to the right of the trail near the big tree.

Another site similar to this configuration has three cairns but the trail tree is located about 100 yards to the west of the site. These three cairns also point in a southeasterly direction. At another site, there are four rock cairns arranged in a square pattern but no trail tree was found in that location; however, this site may have been a campsite as it has good water and flat terrain. Because of the good water at the site, it became a moonshine making site in during the 1940s to 1970s.

Two other sites in north Georgia are worthy of mentioning. One was the site of a small Cherokee village where many trail trees are still located today.

Figure 9-3 Cairns Forming Snake Pattern

Not far from the village site are a number of cairns arranged in a snake-like pattern with one other cairn located away from the snake formation. Figure 9-3 shows a picture of this structure. There are six cairns in the snake pattern which is on a small hill in a mountain basin. A center bearing of the snake pattern points at about 135 degrees which when extended intersects with the location of the Indian village.

At another site on the side of a hill is a formation of rock cairns in a circular pattern with several cairns forming a spoke pointing downhill. The circle of cairns is approximately forty to fifty feet in diameter and downhill from the location is a suspected Indian grave site that was disturbed by a developer and little can be found of it today.

Figure 9-4 Arkansas Rock Cairn Along Indian Trail

In Arkansas, a similar site has been located with multiple rock cairns and other rock formations adjacent to Indian trails and co-located with Indian trail trees. Figure 9-4 shows one of the typical rock cairns located at this site. Figure 9-5 shows a larger cairn near a rock wall that may be part of a ceremonial site. This site is located on a westerly slope of a mountain overlooking a river. The old trail goes right by the site.

Figure 9-5 Large Cairn in Arkansas

Throughout the United States and Canada, rock cairns have been associated with trails. In northwestern New Mexico in the El Malpais National Conservation Area the Indians developed routes across the lava for trade and ceremonial purposes. Rocks were piled to mark their routes across the rugged flows. The Zuni-Acoma Trail of today was highly used for travel between the pueblos of Zuni and Acoma. The Spanish also used this route when they arrived in the 1500s.

The Native American Netroots organization under publisher Neeta Lind said in an article on American Indian sacred places,

"*The Lolo Trail in Montana and Idaho was marked with rock cairns. Nez Perce travelers following the trail would pause to speak to the spirits and to add stones. On their return from the Pacific Ocean in 1806, Lewis and Clark and the Corps of Discovery was led through the Bitterroot Mountains via the Lolo Trail by three Nez Perce guides. At one point, the guides stopped the group at a large cairn of rocks on a ridge top. In spite of the pleas of Lewis and Clark to continue the journey, the Nez Perce insisted that they must stop here for a pipe ceremony to offer their gratitude to the spirit world and to give thanks for their safe passage. Captain Clark noted that the conical mound of stones was six to eight feet in height. The Nez Perce refer to this area as "the Smoking Place.*[93]"

©JACKIE CORDELL, USED WITH PERMISSION

Figure 9-6 shows a picture taken on Spruce Mountain in New York State where a trail tree is located at the site of a rock cairn.

Figure 9-6 Spruce Mountain, New York Tail Near Rock Cairn

Also in the northeast is the 860-acre George B. Parker Woodland owned by the Audubon Society in Coventry, Rhode Island, which consists of majestic old forest, brooks, fields and one hundred mysterious rock cairns. These cairns are located on a trail associated with the Woodland. Their originator is unknown but may have been the Narragansett Indians from that area.

Some of the rock cairns discovered are configured as a pile of rock in lieu of a cylindrical structure. These seem to have more of a ceremonial purpose than marking a trail or being related to the trail. Near York, Maine, the Pennacook Indians have claimed that a large stone structure of many stones located on Mount Agamenticus is the burial site for a seventeenth century Chief Passaconaway, Son of the Bear. When the Indians gather at the site for a ceremony, they add a rock to the pile. Gail Courey Toensing of the *Indian County Today* internet newspaper wrote an article of the conflict between the locals who want to take down the rock pile and the Indians who consider this a sacred site.[94] The fact that the Pennacook Indians have claimed the rock pile in Maine as a sacred site is supported in a report by David Bushnell, *Native Cemeteries and Forms of Burial East of the Mississippi* published in *Bureau of American Ethnology Bulletin*[71]. Bushnell stated,

> *"As early as 1720 some English traders saw a large heap of stones on the east side of the Westenhook or Housatonic River, so called, on the southerly end of the mountain called Monument Mountain, between Stockbridge and Great Barrington. This circumstance gave rise to the name which has ever since been applied to the mountain, a prominent landmark in the valley. This ancient pile of stones may have marked the grave of some great man who lived and died before the coming of the colonists.[95]"*

Hundreds of other rock cairn sites could be discussed here but we think the point has been made that rock cairns, Indian trail trees and Indian trails are related and that when you find one artifact, you may find one or more of the others.

FISH WEIRS

Fish weirs are found mostly in locations were Indian villages existed. Fish have been a major staple of the Indian diet for centuries, and Indians were skilled in harvesting them for the welfare of the entire tribe. Trails were constructed to connect the fish weirs to the village sites but not all fish weirs were close to the villages, necessitating long trails to transport the harvested fish. Since these trails were mostly localized to the villages, it is doubtful that there was a need for marker trees or rock cairns to mark the trails and none have been found.

Building and using fish weirs were common practices to all indigenous peoples. They have been found in Europe, Asia, North America, New Zealand, Micronesia, and many other locations. Some of these fish weirs date to 1000 to 3000 BCE whereas the ones still being found in the rivers of the United States today are considered to be much younger in age.

Anne Frazer Rogers of Western Carolina University presented her findings on fish weirs in the *2008 Appalachian Cultural Resources Workshop Papers*. She stated,

> "In the Southern Appalachian area, there is evidence of the use of weirs in a number of rivers and streams. While the dates at which these weirs were first constructed is impossible to determine, their widespread distribution is an indication of their previous utility. They are found in the Appalachian Mountains of North Carolina, Tennessee, Virginia, and Georgia. In southwestern Virginia and upper east Tennessee, they have been reported in the Clinch and Holston rivers. In North Carolina, they are found in the Nantahala River at Standing Indian Campground, in the Hiawassee River near Murphy, in the Little Tennessee near the Cowee Mound site, and in several places in the Tuckaseegee River.[96] "

In Georgia, the Etowah River begins in the northeastern part of the state and crosses the state in a westerly direction through what was once the Cherokee Nation. In the forty-five mile section of the river from Lake Allatoona near Marietta to Rome, Georgia, there are thirty-six fish weirs probably built by the Cherokees and Creeks who occupied that area in the 1700s and 1800s. Upstream from the lake, in a fifteen mile section of the river near Canton, Georgia, there are another five fish weirs and more are located upstream from those weirs.

Figure 9-7 Etowah Mounds V-Shaped Fish Weir

Near Cartersville, Georgia, on the Etowah River are the Etowah Indian Mounds dating to the Mississippian period. Also nearby was the Cherokee village of Hightower (English translation of Etowah) which was there until the removal of 1838. Directly opposite the mounds is a fish weir which has probably been in use by Indians since the 1100's. Figure 9-7 shows this stone structure V-shaped weir. Near this site, there are five major Indian Trails that junction at Cartersville, Georgia heading north-south and east-west. Perhaps some Indians used these trails to access the fish weirs along the Etowah River. Figure 9-8 shows another stone V-Shaped weir on the Etowah near Canton, Georgia. The weirs on the Etowah River are of stone construction with various shapes including the V-shape configuration. The Indians would drive the fish to the center of the weir structure to capture the fish in a basket. Bill Frazier has done extensive research in Georgia on fish weirs and has documented hundreds of them.[97]

Most of the fish weirs located in the United States are either of stone construction or stake construction with woven branches between the stakes. The stone weirs are usually used in riverine applications whereas the easier stake weirs were used in tidal applications. Allen Lutins, in his thesis for a Masters Degree, made an exhaustive study of fish weirs and reported,

> *"Based on observations from Alaska, Australia, Japan, and southern Africa, weirs seem to conform to one of three basic designs: The first is the tidal weir. The second is a 'maze-like' arrangement of walls; the design is such that fish easily find their way in, but*

can not easily escape. This design is usually used in estuarine areas, and so may be defined as a type of tidal weir. The third is an obstructing wall which funnels fish to a particular point at which they may be trapped or removed. This is the form used in all riverine structures. While conforming to these three basic designs, weirs are constructed with a great diversity of specific shapes and materials.[98]"

Little was known or written about fish weirs in the United States until the 1800s. Lewis and Clark on their famous expedition in 1804-1806 encountered a fish weir near an Indian village in now Idaho where the Lemhi and Salmon Rivers join. J. Wilmer Rigby reported in an article for the Lemhi County Historical Committee that

"William Clark wrote a description of the fish weir and sketched it in great detail."[99]

After the Indians were removed from their homelands, the fish weirs fell into disuse and remain so today. Knowledge about the fish weirs was mostly forgotten even for some Indians that remained in their homelands. In 2009, children and adults of the Eastern Band of the Cherokee Indians were reintroduced

to one of the fish weirs on the Tuckasegee River in North Carolina where they experienced the opportunity to learn how to collect fish in the weir just as their ancestors had done.

Figure 9-8 Stone V-Shaped Weir on the Etowah River near Canton, Georgia

Reporter Becky Johnson of the *Smoky Mountain News*, Waynesboro, North Carolina, captured this event in the July 2009 newspaper edition. She reported,

> *"A ten year old Cherokee student stood on the shore eyeing the wide shallow waters of the Tuckasegee River listening to the marching orders for the exercise about to unfold, one word came to mind: awesome. The student had never heard of a fish weir before, but now he was about to walk in his ancestors' footsteps, using the same stone wall his people built centuries ago to once again - hopefully - trap some fish.*[100]*"*

The re-enactment of using a fish weir was sponsored by the Watershed Association of the Tuckasegee River (WATR), who coordinated the event, with funding support from the Cherokee Preservation Foundation, World Wildlife Fund, and the Royal Bank of Canada. Also supporting the effort were biologists with the Cherokee Fish and Wildlife, US Fish and Wildlife, and several volunteers with WATR.

Two dozen Cherokee children got a taste of what their ancestors did centuries before by learning to herd the fish toward the opening in the weir to trap them. During their visit to the fish weir Russ Townsend, the Eastern Band Cherokee Indians Historic Preservation Officer taught the students about how their ancestors used the river to support themselves which included everything from transportation to the gathering of mussel shells that were ground up and mixed with clay for pottery.

The program at the fish weir is but a start on recapturing the cultural history of the Indians for the younger generations before it is all forgotten. Hopefully more of these type programs will be supported in the future.

Chapter 10

INDIAN TREES AND INDIAN TRAILS
A NATIONWIDE
TRANSPORTATION SYSTEM

The average citizen's opinion of Native Americans is built on the image Hollywood has created and writings of authors who consider the Indians savages, uneducated and of less value than a white man.

In fact, this characterization is far from the truth. Before the white man came to the North American continent, the Indians had built a transportation system of trails that went from coast to coast and from north to south. Their knowledge of how best to build a trail to minimize elevation change, crossing of streams and areas covered in brambles would have made the Romans proud. These trails were used by the Indians for trading with other tribes and the settlers, for hunting parties, for gathering of medicinal plants, for war parties and for interconnectivity to their tribal brethren. It was not uncommon for a hunting or war party to head out on the trails for months at a time, to locate where they want to go and to find their way back to their village.

James Malone wrote in *The Chickasaw Nation* published in 1922,

> *"The expression often used with respect to the condition of the country at the time of its discovery, as being a pathless wilderness, has in it scarcely a vestige of truth. The trails or traces of the Indians extended hundreds of miles in all directions and they crisscrossed each other over the whole continent, and over these the Indians constantly traveled continuous trips thousands of miles. The Chickasaws were great travelers and thought nothing of going to the far west, over*

the trails to Mobile on the Gulf, to Savannah and Charleston on the Atlantic, and to the Great Lakes in the far North.[101"]

Many of these trails were mere footpaths while a few were widened to accommodate horses. George W. Featherston-haugh, who was a British geologist and geographer and was a surveyor of the Louisiana Purchase for the United States government, also surveyed parts of the Indian Territory as treaties were enacted. In his journal of August 1837, while traveling in the Cherokee Middle Town areas of North Carolina, he wrote,

"The country was perfectly wild, without any roads but obscure Indian trails almost hidden by shrubs and high grass."[102]

There was some understanding of astronomy, but there were no maps, no compasses, no GPS navigational instruments. And yet the Indians created and found their way through a maze of interconnecting trails. On some trails, the Indians bent trees to provide guideposts to direct their path. Others used slashes on trees or piled up rocks. Whatever the markers used, the Indians knew the way to and from places of interest. The Indians, better than most, knew the value of a good trail system and built it to support their way of life.

British author Hilarie Belloe probably said it best about the value of a road (trail) in his book *The Road* published in 1923. He said,

"Not only is the road one of the great human institutions because it is fundamental to social existence, but also because its varied effect appears in every department of State. It is the Road that determines the sites of many cities (villages) and the growth and nourishment of all. It is the Road which controls the development of strategies and fixes the sites of battle. It is the Road which gives its frame-work to all economic development. It is the Road which is the channel of all trade and, what is more important, of all ideas. In its most humble functions, it is a necessary guide without which progress from place to place would be a ceaseless experiment.[103"]

Many of the trails remained as an eighteen-inch-wide trail, which the Indians would walk in single file for an entire day without a break, until the white man came. First it was the Spanish, the French and the English. For them, some trails had to be widened to accommodate the horses and carts that De Soto and other explorers brought. Then the traders and early missionaries began to venture into the interior of the continent coming from the east coast, Canada and Mexico. The traders brought goods to trade with the Indians and the life style of the Indians began to change as they sold more animal skins for white man's goods. The trails had to be expanded to accommodate pack trains and small carts and wagons and the narrow trails became rough roads. Treaties were signed and with that came permission for the colonists to build roads on top of old Indian trails.

In 1775, Daniel Boone and thirty other woodsmen were hired to improve the trails between the Carolinas and the west. The resulting route reached into the heart of Kentucky and became known as the Wilderness Road. Other trails were cleared also. By the early 1800s, the newly formed United States government was procuring the rights to build expanded roads through the Cherokee, Creek, Chickasaw and Choctaw Nations and others. By 1801, Thomas Jefferson was signing treaties with the Chickasaws and Choctaws to build a postal route from Boone's Wilderness Road to the lower Mississippi River. This road began the Natchez Trace. In 1805, a treaty was signed with the Cherokees to build a road from west of Augusta and Savannah to the areas that became Chattanooga and Knoxville, Tennessee. With each new road built to accommodate wagons and trade, the settlers, even when they were not authorized to settle there, flocked in to the new territory.

Today, many of our roads and railroads are built on top of these old trails. For some, the historical knowledge about the trail has been lost or forgotten; for others of major significance, the nation has designated the routes as historical trails which the traveler can read about at Kiosk's along the way.

Some of the railroads that were built on top of the old trails have now fallen into disuse and the train tracks have been removed turning the railroads back into trails even if they are no longer wilderness trails.

It is important for us as a nation not to lose sight of our early Indian and American Heritage. We need to educate the public about it by researching and recovering that which can be found and preserved for future generations. To that end, the team of WildSouth and Mountain Stewards has begun a nationwide program to locate Indian trails, village sites, and other artifacts, both living and inanimate, that have a story to tell about the early history of this country.

Locating and documenting the living and related inanimate artifacts began in the decade of 2000 with the nationwide program getting its start in early 2007. Because of the close relationship between the trail trees and Indian trails, it was decided to begin the Indian Trails Mapping Program in late 2007. When you find an Indian Trail tree you can sometimes also find the remnants of an Indian trail and finding a trail can lead you to another trail tree. Many of the Indian trails are buried under improved roads, railroads and land disturbance from urban development and farming. But some are still there almost 300 years after they had been abandoned. With advanced geospatial technology, they can be found.

DEVELOPING THE INDIAN TRAIL LOCATING MYTHOLOGY

Documenting Indian Trails is not new to the academic community. In many states, authors have written reports about the Indian trails of their state and have drawn large scale maps (greater than 1:500,000) of their location. In Georgia, for instance, Marion Hemperley, the state cartographer wrote a report on the *Indian Trails of Georgia*[104] and John Goff added to that information is his report.[105] Probably the single most comprehensive report on Indian trails in the eastern United States was done by William Edwards Myers in 1924.[106] All of these early reports are excellent references to the existence of the trails and their general location. However, all of the maps created as part of these reports suffered from the lack of technology at the time they were published. This limited the accuracy of the where the trail was truly located. In general, the maps show known locations. Where the trails passed through between these points, lines were sketched in as best could be determined by the author from the historical information about the trail. With the advanced technology that has become available in the last decade and more particularly in the last five years, very accurate mapping of Indian trails has become possible.

Locating and documenting an Indian trail requires first researching the paper trail, secondly using new technology to plot the trail based on the information found in the research process (the technology trail) and thirdly, doing the ground-truthing or *boots-on-the-ground* to validate, if possible, that the trail is truly where it has been plotted on the maps.

The Paper Trail

It should be stated for those that wish to follow in the footsteps of the Indian trails mappers, that this whole process is a tedious effort requiring more hours than many would want to commit and advanced computer technology that can strain your financial wherewithal.

The paper trail begins in the state and federal archives. Prior to 2000, searching the archives was limited mostly to the academic community or professional researchers who had access to these source files and maps. With the advent of digital technology that has changed. Books, maps, historical reports and other documentation began to be digitized and cataloged by federal and state libraries and more importantly, companies such as Google developed capabilities to digitize books and other historical materials that have been buried in archives for years and put these data on the Internet. This ever-expanding and growing digitization and cataloging processes coupled with the search engines on the internet has opened to the general public what once was limited to a few. Today, armchair researchers can perform global searches for information and with large storage capacity, download to their computer most information they need for a project. These searches can also identify, when necessary, places to visit to seek more information that may not have yet been digitized and made available to the public.

States Included in PLSS

Figure 10-1 Public Land Survey System

The search for Indian trails data is focused on two key sources of information: ancient maps capable of being geo-registered to an earth model such as Google Earth and written descriptions of the trail by travelers who followed the trail and documented its placement in reference to known landmarks that can be found today. Both of these sources are generally needed to accurately document the real location of an Indian trail.

The search for maps containing Indian trail data can be a little daunting so a few words about this effort are necessary. First of all, the states on the east coast of the United States were colonial states that include the original thirteen colonies and five others. These states were not surveyed by the Public Land Survey System (PLSS) which began to survey the states as they were added to the United States on or after the Indians were removed. Figure 10-1 shows these states in white. Thus, the maps for most of the colonial states are of British, French, Spanish origin or early colonial government maps. Many of these maps are held in United States government library collections but some are in foreign collections. Texas is also colored white on map since it was a republic before being entered into the United States and much of its early mapping dates back to those times.

One colonial state is unique in its availability of early maps. Georgia aggressively sought the removal of the Indians from its borders and enacted laws to forcibly take the Indian lands of the Cherokees. On December 20, 1828, the Georgia legislature enacted a series of laws to strip the Cherokees of their rights and force their removal even though the Cherokees were considered under national laws as a separate nation. This led to the US Supreme Court ruling in 1831.[107] The State of Georgia was found to have overstepped its state authority. Nevertheless, Georgia moved forward with a program in 1830–1832 to survey the north Georgia territory of the Cherokees dividing the area into districts, sections and land lots and proceeded to give the land away to the citizens of the State of Georgia. This mapping became known as the Land Lottery of 1832 and for the most part, the Indian trails and roads that existed in 1832 were documented in these surveys. This original survey of north Georgia is still used today in referencing land ownership. Previous Land Lottery surveys were done in 1805

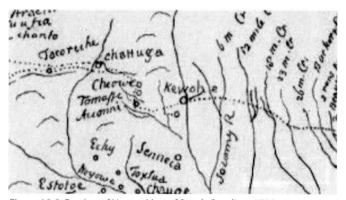

Figure 10-2 Portion of Hunter Map of South Carolina, 1730

through 1827 in the ceding of Creek and Cherokee Indian lands in Georgia.

The states colored in blue in Figure 10-1 were surveyed under the original Government Land Office (GLO) program which began in 1812. Most of those states were surveyed in the 1830s to the 1850s. Those surveys were done under geodetic controlled conditions and are easily georegistered to to-

Figure 10-3 Georgia Land Lottery Map - Georgia , 1821

day land models. The difference in the quality of the maps done under colonial times and GLO or GA Land Lottery maps can be seen in Figure 10-2 and 10-3. In Figure 10-2, the Hunter Map of 1730 shows the location of the Lower Cherokee Towns in South Carolina and a trail going between the towns, but there are no geodetic control lines or landmarks from which the map can be georegistered to an earth model to extract the trails data. Alternatively, the GA Land Lottery map surveyed in 1821, shows the trails and roads and was surveyed under that system of surveying which has lines of control to locate the map section precisely to the earth model

Some of the best data that can be found on Indian trails is in the written accounts of the early settlers that walked or rode a horse along those trails. One such description was provided by Benjamin Hawkins, the US Government agent to the Indians south of Ohio. In the *Letters of Benjamin Hawkins* published by the Georgia Historical Society in 1916, Hawkins described his trip on a portion of the Unicoi Trail which traverses from Travelers Rest in Georgia on the Tugalo River to Fort Loudon in Tennessee. The description of the trail in North Carolina said,

> *"We set out early from our encampment NW; in 16 minutes (he considered 3 miles/hr as his rate for speed) go thro' a narrow pass between two mountains, where probably in some former period the natives must have made a stand in defense of their country. In the center*

of the pass there is a large heap of stones, which must have been placed as a covering to the warriors who lost their lives in defense of the pass; the pass is about 30 ft wide and the ascent on both sides is very steep. In 45 minutes pass a creek running to the left, 8 feet wide; in 19 the path divide just before arrive a large creek, we cross a small one and go down the large one 14 minutes to Little Tellico (A Cherokee village)" [108]

The descriptions of the trails by Hawkins, Featherstonbaugh, and many others who traversed them are very helpful in plotting the trail data on topographic maps of today. British Captain Christopher French's journal writings of 1761, are particularly helpful in determining the location of the Cherokee Trading Path Trail from Ft. Prince George near Keowee Town in western South Carolina to near Clayton, Georgia. The colonial maps of this area shown in Figure 10-2 are not easily geo-registered to allow extraction of trails data from the map.

Captain French was part of the British Regulars involved in the Anglo-Cherokee War during 1758-1761. The Cherokees had attacked Ft. Prince George near Keowee Town in 1760, to attempt to rescue their twenty-nine Cherokee chiefs held prisoner in the fort and they had also attacked Ft. Loudon in Tennessee. The British soldiers, their support troops from South Carolina Provincials and some Indian tribes, wiped out the lower and middle Cherokee towns in 1760-61. By May of 1761, they were again marching toward Ft. Prince George. Captain French kept a detailed journal of his following the Cherokee trading path from the fort to a Cherokee village in Georgia. A small part of his description related to the trading path follows:

*"**Sunday 7th June***

The Army march'd from Fort Prince George; at about Six we passed Keeowee River, which reach'd to the middle, about 5 miles from there we passed another River, call'd the Little River which is Rocky, as also two Creeks at small distances which reach'd to the Knee. At Twelve we reach'd Ocunnih (Oconee) Old Town (12 Miles) formerly a Cherokee settlement, but destroyed by the Creeks. Here we encamp'd, or rather wigwam'd in a Square, having left our Tents behind, excepting two Soldiers Tents of Canvas allow'd for the Officers. This Place is well clear'd & is a fine Country.

Monday 8th June

Marched from Ocunnih Town. At 2 miles crossed Ocunnih Mountain; extremely high and about four miles over, the prospect from it behind was very extensive. Pass'd another hill down which there was a pretty Rivelt; with abundance of waterfalls. At 11 miles crossed Chatuga River which is rapid and pretty broad, it reach'd to the middle (Today, this is called Earl's Ford). Came to a place call'd War Woman Creek which is very rapid & reach'd to the knee. Here the country is very strong having vast high Mountains which command the road all around. About 2 miles further from last ford we crossed War Woman again. At three we reach'd the first part of a place called Tuckahreetchih Old Town about 15 miles from our last encampment.

Tuesday 9th June

March'd about six; soon reach'd the Potatoe Mountains which are extremely high on both sides, & the road narrows, which would make it a great advantage to the enemy. These are about 4 miles through, but no so bad in all parts. At about 10 miles distance is Stickou Old Town, which was destroy'd as other. Here is pretty plain. Here the road turns off to other Middle settlements.

We reach'd Estatowee Old Town about one, after having pass'd one of the finest Spots (a savannah) I ever saw. Soon after our arrival, a party of Indians went upon a scout, & upon their return say'd they had seen many Tracks, & some Fires. This Place is 15 miles from our last Camp. As the runs of water are very numerous in this Country some of us had the Curiosity to count how many we should pass, this day's march they ammount'd to 44." [102]

Using the trail description from French coupled with extracted trail data from colonial maps, the Cherokee trading path can be plotted on topographic maps and its location ascertained by doing boots-on-the-ground survey to located parts of the trail that still exist. After collecting sufficient map and descriptive data on the trails to be located, the next part of the work begins which is technology driven.

Technology of Extracting Trail Data

The technical capability to extract Indian trail data from maps, other than by hand, became available with the advent of Geographic Information Systems (GIS) technology, GPS, digital topographic maps and Google Earth. GIS technology has been around for several decades but its cost limited it to government, universities and private companies. Today, those costs have dropped sufficiently to make it more available to a larger group of researchers.

In 2007, the Mountain Stewards and its partner Wild-South began developing the Indian Trails Mapping Program. That program initiative required software capable of performing the geo-registration of ancient maps and of extracting the trails data though software-enhanced processing techniques. This requires computer processing capabilities generally not resident in normal desktop computers since the file sizes being manipulated are in the gigabyte range and the required storage capacity is in the terabytes. A computer with four dual processors, eight gigabytes of dynamic RAM and video processing along with a terabyte of data storage was built to support the program.

Over a two year period, a mapping methodology was developed, perfected and tested on numerous ancient maps until the process was proven to produce accurate and repeatable results. A discussion of the methodology is detailed in the next section.

Mapping Methodology

The availability of geospatial software is changing how we can use historical maps, narratives, and surveys. These used to be *ball park* documents, but now we can turn many of them

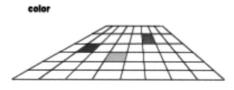

Figure 10-4 Pixel Color Information

into accurate modern maps that can help us locate these historical landmarks with surprising accuracy. What follows is a brief explanation of some of the methods developed to support the Indian Trails Mapping Program.

The Basics

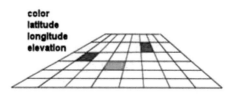

Figure 10-5 Pixel with Coordinate Information

The usual graphic image on your computer is a file with sequential numbers defining the color for each pixel on the screen as seen in Figure 10-4. But there's nothing that says that such a file can't store a lot more information for each pixel–like coordinates (latitude and longitude) and elevation as seen in Figure 10-5. The files would be larger and you would need software to read them.

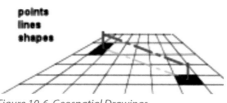

Figure 10-6 Geospatial Drawings

They're called geo-registered image files. You're used to them by now if you use Google Earth or any of the topographic maps that work with your GPS devices.

There are other files, geospatial drawings, which can hold coordinates. They are simply lists of coordinates representing either points, single lines, paths (routes), or simple shapes as shown in Figure 10-6. The software converts these coordinates into points and lines correctly located on your screen.

Figure 10-7 Polygon Data

Another kind of file used in these maps is a table associated with the various shapes in a geospatial drawing. In this example, each state is a separate polygon that has a unique database record – in this case, census data from 1860, showing the population of each state broken down between free men and slaves shown in Figure 10-7. The image is colored-in based on the percentage of slaves in each state. Once the color is associated with the data in the database table, the software automatically puts it in the area of the state on the displayed map of the United States.

There are other kinds of georegistered files – text files that might hold labels with the coordinates for placing them on the map or complex terrain and surface files for displaying 3D information, to mention a few.

One of the powerful features of GIS software is layering. These various kinds of georegistered files can be stacked on top of each other, and since they contain coordinates, they know where to go. In the

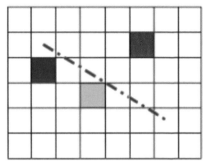

Figure 10-8 Layered Data

displayed image, the layering is invisible, so all the user sees is the line drawn on the image in Figure 10-8.

Rubber Sheeting

Figure 10-9 Henry Mouzon Map of South and North Carolina, 1775

What does all of this have to do with historical maps or surveys? The answer is *everything*! This will be most easily illustrated with an example. Figure 10-9 is the well known 1775 map of South Carolina and eastern North Carolina published by Henry Mouzon. While it is amazingly detailed for its time, one cannot superimpose it on a modern accurate map and use it to locate anything. They were good, but not that good. You can see that there are white labels added all over the map. Figure 10-10 shows a close-up of the labels.

The labels are the coordinates of places that can be identified on modern topographic maps, usually river branching, mountain peaks and other landmarks. These landmarks are

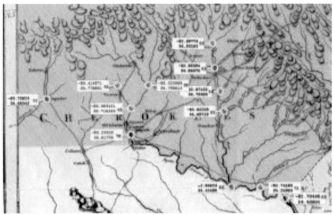

Figure 10-10 Mouzon Map with GPS Labels Added

stable over the 235 years since the map was published. How-ever, locating the same points on the Mouzon map and the modern topographic map is a very tedious process, but it is required in order to adjust the ancient map to match the to-pography accurately. Once sufficient points have been located, usually one hundred or more points, then these points can be entered into a table that's associated with this image being pro-cessed in the geospatial software.

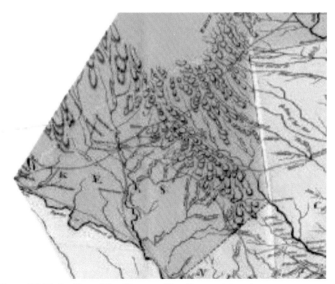

Figure 10-11 Section of the Mouzon Map Geo-registered

Some of the best software available today to perform the geospatial data processing of image files is ArcView developed by ESRI Software. However, ArcView and all of its extensions have a cost that can be beyond the means of many researchers and there is a significant learning curve for the software. For the researchers with limited funding, however, Manifold® software can perform all the needed software functions at a cost

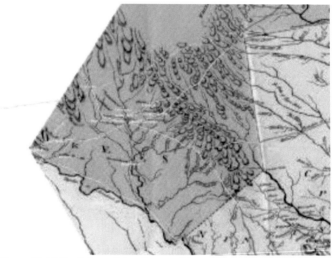

Figure 10-12 Trails Data Being Extracted from Map

less than than ArcView. Therefore, the software chosen for our program was Manifold.

The computer software builds a model from the geospatial points and uses the model to stretch and pull the image using a variety of mathematical algorithms until these points are correctly placed on a coordinate grid that matches the true topographic earth model. The resultant map image is now *georegistered* and can easily be superimposed on the modern map with 235 years of inaccuracies effectively erased.

Figure 10-11 shows a small section of the Mouzon map that has been stretched to fit the true earth model. Because of the size of the image files and the complexity of the processing, it has been found that the map, in some cases, had to be broken into smaller sections in order for the processing to be accurate enough. This is a trial-and-error process wherein the map is stretched and compared to the earth model for accuracy. If it does not meet standards, then more points must be added to the model in order to achieve the required accuracy.

Figure 10-13 New Map with Old and New Data Combined

After the required accuracy is achieved, then the next step can be taken. At first, looking at the map, it's tempting to think of it as distorted, but the opposite is the case. The map is now *undistorted* and usable. This is a long slow process, but well-worth the effort. It's now a simple process to overlay the *undistorted* map on top of Google Earth and begin to trace the trails, the roads, villages and other landmarks from the map onto a blank drawing as shown in Figure 10-12. The resulting *drawing file* can then be displayed in Google Earth or on a topographic map as well as in any GIS program.

Once the data is extracted from the ancient map, a new map can be built using layers from the map plus other layers of data desired to be included in the map. Figure 10-13 is a typical new map with the old data included with new geospatial layers. The background image layer is from the National Elevation Database. The next layer up has a River drawing from the National Hydrology Database. The next layer is the State Borders drawing, the Roads from our geo-referenced Mouzon Map, the Towns from that map, and finally the Town Name labels. These same files (after a change of format) could be overlaid on a detailed topographic map to use for archeological exploration or ground truthing. They can be overlaid in Google Earth or Microsoft Virtual Earth which use aerial photographs. Another of the beauties of this method is that the coordinates can be saved, and anything that is located can be added to the collection of points, improving the map's accuracy.

PLSS AND GEORGIA LAND LOTTERY SURVEYS

The survey maps created under the government Public Land Survey System (PLSS) and the Georgia Land Lottery were done using more precise surveying methodology than that used for the early maps of the colonial states. Although some mistakes were made by the surveyors, (e.g. the location of the border between Tennessee and Georgia is still in dispute), these maps are easily geo-registered to the earth models so extraction of Indian trails data is more easily accomplished compared to ancient colonial maps. Further, all land transactions of today are based on these surveys.

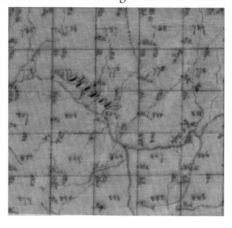

Figure 10-14 Land Lottery Survey Map

Typically the PLSS divides land into six-mile-square townships, and the townships are further divided into thirty-six one-mile sections. These one-mile sections are then divided into quarter and quarter-quarter sections. A one-mile square section contains 640 acres of land. The range is a north-south column of townships surveyed from an initial point in Glasgow, Pennsylvania. All surveys are related to the initial point through vertical meridian lines, a total of thirty-seven, and horizontal base lines.

The Georgia Land Lottery System of surveying was similar to the PLSS in that the land was divided into Sections going north-south which were further divided into Districts by horizontal lines and the districts were further sub-divided into Land Lots. There were seven Land Lotteries in Georgia. The first five land lotteries (1805, 1807, 1820, 1821 and 1827) redistributed the Creek and Cherokee lands that had been ceded to the state. The sixth and seventh land lotteries in 1832, forcibly took the Cherokee lands and gave it to citizens of Georgia. The second 1832 land lottery gave away land used during the Georgia Gold Rush, although the government did not guarantee that there was any gold left on the lots. The land lots distributed from the 1832 surveys were forty acres for a Gold Lot and 160 acres for a normal Land Lot. In the Creek surveys, the Land Lots varied from 202.5 acres to 490 acres.

The surveyors of the PLSS and Georgia Lottery maps done in the early to mid 1800s were paid sparingly for their efforts to trek through wilderness areas of the country to map the area. Their principal job was to establish boundaries and corner points of land plots and to record other landmarks as time permitted. Thus, some Indian trails were recorded but not all. Figure 10-14 shows a section of a Georgia Land Lottery map where the Indian trails were recorded. There are large sections of these maps where little other than the boundaries and corners were mapped.

©2010 GOOGLE IMAGE USDA FARM SERVICE AGENCY, ©EUROPA TECHNOLOGIES

Figure 10-15 1832 Georgia land Lottery Survey with Indian Trails

Figure 10-15 shows the entire 1832 Georgia Land Lottery Survey with the Indian trails highlighted. As can be seen in the figure, not all the trails are connected together indicating

Figure 10-16 Georgia-Alabama Indian Trails from Lottery and PLSS Surveys

parts of the map where the surveyors failed to plot the trails information on a Land Lot. Some of the missing data can be recovered by doing ground surveys of the trails to locate the data if the land has not been disturbed to remove remnants of the trail. However, in many cases, farming and urban developments have removed these traces from existence. In those cases, judgments have to be made as to where the trail may have been located to connect missing trail segments.

Figure 10-16 shows the Indian trails extracted from PLSS Alabama (1840) and Georgia Land Lottery (1820-1832) surveys and plotted in Google Earth. In almost all cases, the trails were coincident across state lines.

The culmination of geo-registering PLSS , Georgia Lottery and colonial maps is shown in Figure 10-17 where the Indian trails from each source are plotted in Google Earth. The system of trails that were build by the Indians centuries ago begin to reappear and show the extensiveness of this transportation system before it was partially lost after the Indian removal.

INTEGRATED MAPPING PROGRAM METHODOLOGY

Once the Indian trails and other data have been extracted from the source maps, the process of validating these data and building of useful maps can begin. Figure 10-18 graphically portrays that methodology. The extracted data from maps

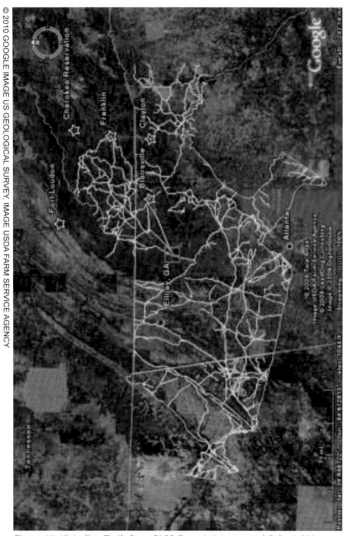

Figure 10-17 Indian Trails from PLSS Georgia Lottery and Colonial Maps

overlaid on Google Earth is in a GPS file format known as a *kml* file which is compatible with Google Earth but not other topographic programs or GPS devices. It, therefore, has to be converted to other formats to make it compatible with the other software or hardware. Thus, the KML editor was developed to easily convert the data from Google Earth to topographic program formats and for inserting into handheld GPS

Figure 10-18 Integrated Mapping Methodology

devices. Likewise field data collected by GPS devices can also be converted to be compatible with Google Earth if needed. Today, however, Google Earth and most topographic programs can read the data directly from the GPS devices. With this integrated capability in hand, the researchers can proceed to validate extracted data in boots-on-the-ground surveys to locate the true position of the trails. Because of some variations in geospatial data used in the surveys, the trails can be off by as much as several tenths of a mile so validation is necessary to correct these potential errors.

Figure 10-19 Cherokee Path West of Oconee Town 2010

GROUND – TRUTHING AND VALIDATION

The easiest way to describe the process of ground-truthing, boots-on-the-ground the trails and other archaeological important sites is to show by example how this works on an existing trail.

The Cherokee Trading Path began in Charleston, SC, and headed in a westerly direction to where Keowee Town, a Cherokee Lower

Figure 10-20 Westerly Cherokee Path in South Carolina

Town of the early 1700s, was located in now Oconee County, South Carolina. From Keowee Town the path continued in a more northwest direction until it crossed over Little River and continued on to Oconee Town. From there it then went over the mountains toward current Clayton, Georgia. Other paths went from Oconee Town NW over Oconee Mountain and then north to Highlands and Franklin, NC. Both of these paths eventually ended in the Cherokee villages of North Carolina and Tennessee. Figure 10-19 shows the extracted Cherokee Path in red west of Oconee Town and Oconee Station, a government outpost built in 1792. Using these data, points (waypoints) can then be found on Google Earth where the trail crosses a known landmark such as a road, river, etc. With these waypoints loaded into a GPS device, the waypoint can be highlighted and using the GPS *GOTO* function, the researcher can follow the map and direction on their GPS screen to locate the waypoints on the earth. If the trail still exists at or near this point, it can be found. The blue line in Figure 10-19 shows a section of the Cherokee Path that was discovered to exist almost coincident with the trail extracted from a colonial map. The yellow line on the map represents another trail also located at the site of Oconee Station known to have existed. This trail heads south to the Cherokee village of Tugalo on the Tugalo River between Georgia and South Carolina. This area of South Carolina has had little land disturbance with large acreages of land being preserved by the state and federal government. Thus, Indian trails in these areas are more likely to be found.

Figure 10-21 Marker Tree at Shallow Ford River Crossing

Using the same process described above for the Cherokee Trading Path, other Cherokee Trails were also located where it crossed a highway in a state forest area. Again the red line in the Figure 10-20 is the extracted trail data and the blue line shows where the trail location was confirmed.

The final validation of these trails was done in 2009-2011 where researchers walked sections of the trails that had been found using a GPS to record the exact trail location. These data will then be used to update the trail location of the final maps showing the Cherokee trails. In some locations on major trails that cross over rivers, trail trees can be found marking the shallow ford crossing points. Figure 10-21 shows a bent tree marking a crossing point on the Chattooga River between South Carolina and Georgia. Also near this location the old roadbed of the trail which was expanded to accommodate pack horses and wagons

Figure 10-22 Cherokee Path Near Chattooga River

was found to still exist as shown in Figure 10-22.

In researching the location of trails, especially when the trail isn't found at the GPS location being plotted, it is good to keep in mind how the Indians created trails. Trails usually took the path of least resistance so going over mountains, the path would have most often followed ridge lines. The path would have also avoided low areas where there are swampy conditions, brambles and heavy vegetation. The path would also pass by water sources and shelter locations as these were needed to support the Indians on their long treks. The trail trees are also a good indicator of where a trail may be located.

Ellsworth Jaeger in his book *Wildwood Wisdom* published in 1945 provides a lot of good information about Indian trails learned from many years of interviewing the Indians about their woodland knowledge.[110] His book contains pictures of some of the trail trees found in the central United States in the early part of the 1900s.

THE WESTERN TRAILS

In the western states, particularly in the Southwest, there are few trees to mark the location of trails, and yet we know the Indians traversed these areas regularly. Some trails are marked with rock cairns that remain today to guide a person on the pathway. However, because there are a lot of areas consisting of rock and desert areas of shifting sands, locating a worn trail is difficult although the southwest Indians have followed trails for centuries. For the areas of the Southwest in Arizona, Nevada and Utah there are signs that marked these trails that have recently been found. Bob Ford spent years researching petroglyphs in Arizona and made an amazing discovery in 1996 about some of the glyphs. He published his findings on the internet in 1997, which was entitled the *Water Trails of the Anasazi*.[111] Ford found a number of identical petroglyphs that seem to mark a trail across the Arizona Strip by the early inhabitants, the Anasazi Indians. The petroglyph had a distinctive shape which was named by Ford as the Water Glyph since his research showed these glyphs not only indicated the direction of the trail but they also led the traveler to water locations, a very necessary commodity in the southwest.

The Water glyph, shown in Figure 10-23, is a circle with a line drawn through it pointing in the direction of the trail and water. Water glyphs are usually forty-eight inches long by twenty-four inches wide, with grooves carved half an inch to an inch deep. Some of the circles have a dot in the circle and in some the dot is outside the circle. The meaning of this dot is not known at this time.

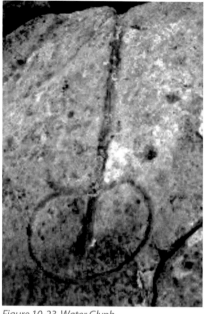

Figure 10-23 Water Glyph

Ford pointed out in his research of the Water Glyphs,

"The single most important factor while traveling across the Arizona Strip was, and still is, where to get water next." [111]

The Arizona Strip covers Northern Arizona, Southern Utah and Southeastern Nevada. Ford spent a great deal of time locating and photographing the Water Glyphs in *the Strip* and finally concluded these had to mark a trail and water. His findings were further reinforced by written journal accounts of Major John Wesley Powell. Powell surveyed the Arizona Strip in 1871, and used Paiute Indian guides to assist him in his expedition of this area of northwestern Arizona that is somewhat isolated from the remainder of Arizona by the Colorado River. Ford reported that Powell mentioned in his survey notes that from time to time, their guide would leave the group, ascend some butte or bluff, scout around for awhile looking at the ground and then the horizon, come back and announce simply "we travel this way to find water." [111] Obviously, the Paiute Indian was reading the Water Glyph signs. More can be found about the Powell Expeditions in the southwestern United States in Frederick Dellen-baugh and John Powell's written accounts in *A Canyon Voyage: The Narrative of the Second Powell Expedition Down The Green-Colorado River From Wyoming, 1871-1872.*[112]

Based on his findings, Ford recruited Dixon Spendlove, another amateur archaeologist to help in the exploration to further develop the theory of the Water Glyphs. Their efforts led to locating many more of the glyphs and confirmation that they seemed to all point to the next glyph in an alignment of a probable trail. Together, they have identified over one hundred twenty-eight of the Water Glyphs in three states which was the homelands of the Anasazi centuries ago. The result of their findings has led to the capability of a person to be able to cross the entire Arizona Strip from House Rock Valley in Arizona on the east, to Beaver Dam in Nevada on the west finding water sources along the way. Ford and Spendlove's work has led to other studies of this amazing finding which undoubtedly will continue for the years to come.

Throughout the 1800s, many trails were opened across the western United States. As with the trails in the eastern United States, most of these western trails were first walked by the Indians. Thus, it was common for many Native Americans to serve as scouts and guides for the trading companies, the railroads, the Army and for private individuals and groups. One notable scout and guide was Black Beaver who was a Lenape (Delaware) Indian. He could speak English, French, Spanish, and about eight different Indian languages and use Indian sign language. Helen Holton, Black Beaver's great-great granddaughter said,

"From a young age Black Beaver was trained to take note of the smallest signs, human or animal."[113]

He knew trail craft and could use it to find his way along any Indian trail existing. Black Beaver spent over fifty years guiding groups throughout the west from Canada to Mexico and from the Mississippi River to the Pacific Ocean. Like the eastern trails, the western trails were extensive covering the entire western United States.

Chapter 11

PRESERVATION OF THE "LIVING ARTIFACTS"

INTRODUCTION

Across the globe, many countries have made commitments and have taken legislative actions to preserve their historic cultural sites and artifacts including those related to the aboriginal peoples who occupied the lands before other settlers moved in. However, for most countries, the legislative action taken didn't occur until late in the twentieth century long after many sites were destroyed or robbed of their artifacts and sacred objects by treasure hunters. In some countries, efforts are continuing to preserve the cultural heritage while in others, including the United States, the overall applied effort to preserve the historical and cultural aspects of the country, particularly those related to the aboriginal people, is not only lacking government leadership and action, but in some cases, sacred sites and artifacts are being destroyed in spite of what had been promised in long standing treaties. Unfortunately, big business and development interests seem to almost always trump the preservation laws.

After many years of government neglect, in 1968, a few Indian nations formed the American Indian Movement (AIM) to address various issues concerning the Native American community including poverty, housing, treaty issues, and police harassment. To make their points known, they seized the Bureau of Indian Affairs in 1972 in Washington, DC, to protest the neglect. However, this protest didn't seem to register with the country's legislators because in 1978, the Ninety-fifth Congress introduced eleven legislative bills to abolish treaties with Indian tribes of the United States. This congressional action resulted in AIM creating the 1978 Longest Walk, a now famous 3,600 mile march to Washington, DC, to protest the legislative actions. The Longest Walk resulted in the congressional planned action to abolish treaties being defeated thus protecting the remaining pieces of native sovereignty. This activism contributed to the passage of the American Indian Religious Freedom Act of 1978.

Some improvement of relationships between the United States and tribal governments occurred throughout the 1980s culminating in the enactment of the Native American Graves and Repatriation Act of 1990 which requires federal agencies and museums receiving federal funds to locate, inventory and determine the ultimate disposition of cultural items, that is, Native American human remains, funerary objects, sacred objects and objects of cultural patrimony under their possession or control. While progress is still being made, there remain many issues worldwide surrounding the rights of the aboriginal peoples.

On September 30, 2007, the United Nations General Assembly adopted the Declaration on the Rights of Indigenous Peoples. This Declaration provided for the indigenous peoples the chance to have their rights recognized. Some of their rights include rights to self-determination, traditional lands and territories, traditional languages and customs, natural resources and sacred sites. Most would simply view these as basic human rights. 144 signatories voted in favor of the declaration; four did not including the United States, Canada, Australia and New Zealand. These four countries, especially Canada and Australia, had been out in front enacting policies and laws to protect the artifacts and aboriginal people's sacred sites. Why they refused to sign such an important declaration is testimony to these countries not making a full commitment to protect the cultural artifacts of the native peoples.

AIM sponsored a thirtieth anniversary walk in July 2008, this one 8,200 miles, beginning in San Francisco Bay and ending in Washington, DC' to present a list of demands which included again the need to protect sacred sites and for improvements in Native American sovereignty.

Individual tribes have continued to work with the United States government to right longstanding wrongs. For some, their patience has run out. A delegation of Lakota Sioux delivered a declaration of secession from the United States to the US State Department in December 2007. Citing many broken treaties by the US government in the past and the loss of vast amounts of territory originally awarded in those treaties, the group announced its intentions to form a separate nation within the United States known as the Republic of Lakotah. Bill Harlan reported in the *Rapid City Journal* on December 12, 2007, that,

> *"Russell Means and other members of the Lakota tribe have renounced treaties and are withdrawing from the United States. We are now a free country and independent of the United States of America."* [114]

Part of this issue stems from the Lakota claim that the US government stole lands guaranteed to them in treaties and those lands have not been returned. A US Supreme Court decision awarded the Lakota $122 million dollars in 1980 for the lands but the Lakota refused the settlement.

THE UNITED STATES PRESERVATION LAWS

There are three laws that frame the government requirements for preservation of cultural heritage in the United States. These are the National Historic Preservation Act (NHPA) of 1966 (Public Law 89-665), the Archaeological Resources Protection Act (ARPA) of 1979 (Public Law 96-95) and the Native American Graves Protection and Repatriation Act (NAGPRA) (Public Law 101-601). Collectively, these laws provide protection of cultural Indian sites including sacred sites and all artifacts that are found on public and Indian properties or involve projects funded by federal funds.

The spirit and intent of these laws can be summarized by the purpose of the NHPA which states in part:

(b) The Congress finds and declares that —

> *(1) the spirit and direction of the Nation are found-*
> *ed upon and reflected in its historic heritage;*
>
> *(2) the historical and cultural foundations of the*
> *Nation should be preserved as a living part of*
> *our community life and development in order*
> *to give a sense of orientation to the American*
> *people;*
>
> *(3) historic properties significant to the Nation's*
> *heritage are being lost or substantially altered,*
> *often inadvertently, with increasing frequency;*
>
> *(4) the preservation of this irreplaceable heritage*
> *is in the public interest so that its vital legacy*
> *of cultural, educational, aesthetic, inspiration-*
> *al, economic, and energy benefits will be main-*
> *tained and enriched for future generations of*
> *Americans.*

The NHPA establishes the function of a State Historic Preservation Officer (SHPO) and was later amended to add a similar function for tribal lands of Tribal Historic Preservation
Officer (THPO). The SHPO is mandated by the NHPA to
represent the interests of the state when consulting with federal agencies under Section 106 of the NHPA and to maintain
a database of historic properties. The NHPA also created the
Advisory Council on Historic Preservation (ACHP), an inde-
pendent federal agency in the executive branch that oversees
the Section 106 review process. In addition to the views of
the agency, the SHPO and the ACHP, input from the general public and Native American tribes is also required. The re-
sponsibilities of all parties in the Section 106 review process
are set forth in federal regulations developed by the ACHP as
36 CFR 800: Protection of Historic Properties.

The ARPA stated in its purpose and findings in Section 2
that:

(a) The Congress finds that—

> *(1) archaeological resources on public lands and Indian lands are an accessible and irreplaceable part of the Nation's heritage;*

> *(2) these resources are increasingly endangered because of their commercial attractiveness;*

> *(3) existing Federal laws do not provide adequate protection to prevent the loss and destruction of these archaeological resources and sites resulting from uncontrolled excavations and pillage; and*

> *(4) there is a wealth of archaeological information which has been legally obtained by private individuals for noncommercial purposes and which could voluntarily be made available to professional archaeologists and institutions.*

(b) The purpose of this Act is to secure, for the present and future benefit of the American people, the protection of archaeological resources and sites which are on public lands and Indian lands, and to foster increased cooperation and exchange of information between governmental authorities, the professional archaeological community, and private individuals having collections of archaeological resources and data which were obtained before October 31, 1979 (the date of the enactment of this Act).

The ARPA goes on to state in Section 3 that the definition of an archaeological resource is:

> *(1) the term "archaeological resource" means any material remains of past human life or activities which are of archaeological interest, as determined under uniform regulations promulgated pursuant to this Act. Such regulations containing such determination shall include, but not be limited to: pottery, basketry, bottles, weapons, weapon projectiles, tools, structures or*

portions of structures, pit houses, rock paintings, rock carvings, intaglios, graves, human skeletal materials, or any portion or piece of any of the foregoing items. Non-fossilized and fossilized paleontological specimens, or any portion or piece thereof, shall not be considered archaeological resources, under the regulations under this paragraph, unless found in an archaeological context. No item shall be treated as an archaeological resource under regulations under this paragraph unless such item is at least 100 years of age.

Thus, it can be seen by the current laws for archaeological resources and preservation of cultural heritage, the living artifacts of trail/marker trees or culturally modified trees and the related artifacts of rock cairns or fish weirs are not included in the law and are not protected even though they are considered by some Indians as being sacred sites.

Seemingly the spirit and intent of these preservation laws along with federal mandated officers to protect them would be enough. However, President Clinton had to sign *Executive Order 13007* on 24 May, 1996, to provide unrestricted access to sacred sites by the Indians. That order stated in part:

Section 1. Accommodation of Sacred Sites.

(a) In managing Federal lands, each executive branch agency with statutory or administrative responsibility for the management of Federal lands shall, to the extent practicable, permitted by law, and not clearly inconsistent with essential agency functions,

(1) accommodate access to and ceremonial use of Indian sacred sites by Indian religious practitioners and

(2) avoid adversely affecting the physical integrity of such sacred sites. Where appropriate, agencies shall maintain the confidentiality of sacred sites.

PRESERVATION OF ARTIFACTS AND SACRED SITES

In Chapter 8 and 9, we addressed some of the desecration of sacred sites of the Indigenous peoples on the North America continent. Similar statements can be made about the actions being undertaken in other countries as well. The laws and policy are in place to protect the cultural heritage of the Indians but adequate and full implementation of those laws is lacking. There isn't a single day that goes by that a sacred site or artifact isn't being destroyed or at least impacted.

Today, there are web sites that list the multitude of sites that are under attack by development or other activities. Sue Sturgis of The Institute of Southern Studies wrote in their on-line magazine in September 2009,

> "A re-consecration ceremony was held this past weekend at a damaged Indian mound in Oxford, AL. As we reported last month, the 1,500-year-old sacred and archaeologically significant site was partially demolished during a taxpayer-funded economic development project, with the excavated dirt to be used as fill for construction of a Sam's Club, a retail warehouse store owned by Wal-Mart." [115]

She went on to report of a multitude of other Wal-Mart projects where Indian sacred sites were impacted.

A project in Macon County, North Carolina, to extend the runway for the Macon County Airport Authority in 2009 clearly shows that the current laws and those that are responsible to uphold them are not working adequately. The Macon County Airport Authority filed an Environmental Impact Statement (EIS) as required by law for extending their runway a distance of five hundred feet. Under the EIS they performed an archaeological check of the site. However, had the State Historic Preservation Officer (SHPO) done their job, they would have known that this site was the location of the Cherokee Middle Town Lotla. Also it was on the Cherokee Trading Path from Charleston to the Cherokee Middle Towns. This site is of significant cultural and historical importance to the

Cherokees. According to a preliminary archaeological report of the area, evidence of human activities as early as 2 AD remains intact beneath the ground. Hundreds of Native American burials are also interred on the property.

Lamar Marshall, Cultural Heritage Officer for WildSouth, wrote a detailed accounting of everything that was done wrong with the EIS, with the SHPO's management of the project and many other federal laws that were not followed. The end result should have been *Case Closed*, stop the project. But no, the SHPO incredibly recommended that only twenty-five percent of the graves should be moved and the rest paved over. Cherokee Chief Michell Hicks of the Eastern Band of the Cherokee Indians with support of the United Keetoowah Band of the Cherokees Indians in Oklahoma recommended that one hundred percent of the graves would have to be removed which eventually the Airport Authority agreed to after a lot of negotiation. Sadly, this event is an example of an everyday common occurrence across the county with regard to preserving sacred sites.

In 1966, the Congress stated its findings as the need to enact the National Historical Preservation Act (NHPA) that:

> *(2) the historical and cultural foundations of the Nation should be preserved as a living part of our community life and development in order to give a sense of orientation to the American people;*

> *(3) historic properties significant to the Nation's heritage are being lost or substantially altered, often inadvertently, with increasing frequency; Over forty years later, not only can the same findings be stated but they can be further emphasized as a national crisis. Unless action is taken soon, there will be few national and aboriginal historic properties left for the current and future generations.*

WHAT IS REQUIRED TO PRESERVE THE LIVING ARTIFACTS AND SACRED SITES

Probably, the single most important thing that has to happen to solve this ever-increasing problem is the recognition that destruction of sacred sites does exist by all levels of government and by the citizens of this country. The United States historical and cultural heritage belong to everyone, and it is our collective responsibility to see that it is protected and preserved. What actions that are needed to accomplish this goal are delineated in the following list.

1. **Update/change the Current Laws: The NHPA and the APRA laws do not adequately protect the sacred sites and do not cover the living artifacts.** In order for a historic site to be protected, it must be registered under the National Register of Historic Places. Many of the archaeological sites, including the sacred sites, can only be protected if they remain unknown to the general public. Too many sites have been raided by treasure hunters or destroyed by people who, for example, want to carve their names on places where petroglyphs exist. Archaeological sites are often protected today by state and private archaeologists using a numbering system to refer to them and access to the list of where the sites are located is held to a limited few who have a need to know. The sacred sites are a difficult issue. These sites are mostly known only to the tribal elders and disclosure of them could result in their destruction. In a briefing to Congress on this issue in 2002, the Indian leaders stated in a fact sheet prepared by the Morning Star Institute:

   > *"It has been the experience of Native Americans that disclosure about the location, nature or use of sacred place leads to assaults on them. Many of these places are fragile and have been destroyed by too many visitors or vehicles or activities."* [116]

   The second part of this issue is the fact that some sites exist on private lands and the federal laws do not cover this situation. Our privacy rights are upheld in the Constitution and Bill of Rights but, in some cases such as the National Environmental Policy, the rights of the whole population are of greater importance than individual rights. The NHPA and the APRA have to be changed to include policy to protect the rights of the Indians to protect their sacred places that are on private lands. The definition of what is an Archaeological Resource in the APRA law needs to be updated to provide for the protection of the living artifacts.

2. **Develop and Adopt Federal Policy Manuals to Protect Living Artifacts:** The Canadian and Australian governments have enacted policies to protect the living artifacts of the aboriginal peoples, especially the culturally modified trees. They have prepared and published numerous manuals to train government and private enterprise staffs on how to recognize and document the various types of CMTs and how to preserve them. Further, these policies have been used to deal with encroachment issues on sites that contain artifacts to be protected. The federal and state governments can easily adopt and modify these manuals to be used in the United States. Already the managers of many national parks, forests and wilderness areas in the northwestern part of the United States have initiated local efforts to identify and protect the CMTs in their areas of cognizance. This effort needs to be expanded to include the bent trees and to be made a consistent policy nationwide.

3. **Establish a Nationwide Dendrochronology Program to Document the Living Artifacts:** There are doubts in the minds of some that these living artifacts are of Native American origin even though tribal elders have declared them to be. The final proof of their originality can only be ascertained by aging the tree through dendrochronology and through confirmation of the tribal history that shows they occupied that area at the same historical period of the age of the tree.

4. **Establish a Program to Educate the Public about the Living Artifacts:** Protection of the living artifacts can be legislated through government policy and actions by government personnel to carry out that policy. However, like sacred sites, many of these artifacts are on private lands and their protection is in the hands of the landowners. Experience has shown that when properly educated about this historical legacy, landowners will do all in their power to protect the trees. In several locations across the country, whole communities have made it a policy to educate all that live in that area. They have installed signs to identify the living resource and instructed those that visit the site to be respectful of this historical resource.

Finally, to put all of what has been said about protection of these historical legacies into perspective, it might be appropriate to put the shoe on the other foot in a hypothetical news release about Arlington Cemetery in Washington, DC, and what kind of public outcry might result from such an event:

(Hypothetical News Release)

Defense Base Closure and Realignment Commission (BRAC) Announces the Closure of Fort McHenry and its Sale to a Shopping Center Developer

Arlington, VA News Release

The developer, STOMPON, has recently purchased the entire Fort McHenry property from the Defense Department adjacent to Arlington Cemetery. STOMPON plans to build the largest shopping and entertainment center development in the US at the old Army base. The developer's spokesperson said, "This development will include many box stores and an entertainment complex that will be far better than the Six Flags developments currently open in the US." The spokesperson went on to admit that, "The plans for the development will include a monster rollercoaster swinging out over the cemetery. Many of the graves at Arlington Cemetery will be impacted but that really isn't a problem. Funds will be included in the development to move these graves to some other location." The development will certainly be visible on the skyline from many of the Washington DC monuments.

How many complaints would be heard about this hypothetical announcement and how many groups would march on Washington in protest? Ten million or more is probably not out of the question.

Chapter 12

FUTURE OF THE
MYSTERY OF THE TREES

Considering that the Trail Tree Project began only a few short years ago, one would think that there is plenty of time to move ahead at a steady pace to accomplish our goals of documenting and saving the cultural and historical places where the living artifacts are found. However, as pointed out in Chapter 11 and others, time is short if we are going to save any of these trees and places before development or aging of the trees overtakes our efforts to make them speak. Time is of the essence.

TRAIL TREE PROJECT

The Trail Tree Project began nationwide in March 2007, and by 2011, over 1,750 trees had been identified with about 100 trees being added each year. As more people get involved in this effort, the locating and documenting of the trees is accelerating. The number of trees sounds like a lot but it's not. Thousands of trees are known to exist in the United States, especially CMTs that are not documented in the national database but, in some cases, are documented in other databases. In order to show government officials the full extent of this cultural legacy, eventually the various databases will need to share data to be able to present a comprehensive picture.

The team of researchers working on this project is small and needs to expand a hundred-fold. Multiple researchers are needed in every state to fully document the number of trees and other artifacts that should be preserved. Since a number of the CMTs are also located in the Canadian provinces that relate to those found in the United States, some cataloging of these trees should be done to show the northern continent scope of this legacy.

The Mountain Stewards website at www.mountainstew-ards.org has attracted a lot of attention, and the number of hits on the website continues to grow each month with people sending in data on trees that they have found. This is the slower approach to getting the job done but it is nevertheless working.

INDIAN TRAILS

Figure 10-17 shows the extent of Cherokee Indian trails that have been extracted from ancient survey maps and integrated into an Indian trails map covering parts of four states. Creek Indian Trails in middle and south GA and AL are now being extracted and will be added to the database in the near future. Ground-truthing of many of these trails has not yet begun but for those that have, some of the trails are being found where they were expected to be located. In early 2009, the Cherokee Preservation Foundation of the Eastern Band of the Cherokee Indians (EBCI) contracted with the Indian Trails Mapping Team to locate the trails on their Qualla Boundary area, the Great Smoky Mountain National Park and some of the surrounding area where the Cherokee Middle, Overhill and Out Town villages are located. The initial effort of this work was completed in 2010. Further work is now underway continuing through 2012.

The Mapping Team is also working in Oconee, South Carolina, to locate trails associated with the Cherokee Lower Town villages. This work will develop the trails in Oconee and eventually connect to the trails that reach all the way back to Charleston, South Carolina.

Using the trails discovered in the southeast as a base, the program will be continually expanded to fill in each state beginning in the southeast and moving westward along the trails used in the Trail of Tears. Prior to the Indian removal, many of the trails that were used for that atrocious event were old Indian Trails. These trails had been used for hunting and trading with tribes in the mid-west and far west. War parties also used these trails.

There is a great deal of ground-truthing that has to be done to validate the location of the trails that has been extracted from the maps to date. Teams of researchers equipped with handheld GPS will be required to check these trails in the southeast and their field data will be used to correct the mapped trails. Also, in places where the surveyors did not connect two or more segments of the trails together, some research will be needed to determine if the missing sections of the trails can be found and documented. Hopefully, some of this trail work can assist archaeology teams in their efforts to locate Indian villages and other sites important to the Native Americans so that they can be identified and preserved.

The final product of these efforts will be the publishing of Indian Trail maps where appropriate and the designation of some of the more important trails as National Historic Trails under the National Trails System Act of 1968. This act promotes the network of scenic, historic, and recreation trails that provide for outdoor recreation needs, promote the enjoyment, appreciation, and preservation of open-air, outdoor areas and historic resources, and encourage public access and citizen involvement.

DOCUMENTARY

As of 2011, there are over eighty hours of video-taped interviews with tribal elders and old timers who have shared parts of the story about the trees and their mystery. Also there are many hours of background video to be used to stitch together this very important story about the legacy of the Native Americans. When funding becomes available from foundation grants or other contributions, the *Mystery of the Trees* documentary will be finished for showing on public television outlets. This was started as a one-hour documentary. As the story unfolded, the need to document more aspects of the story became apparent. The documentary has grown into a two-to-four hour series production.

CHANGING THE NATIONAL LAWS

Chapter 11 detailed the problems with the current laws and what needs to be done to change them. Our Indian brethren have been working on this for a long time with some progress being made. With the persistent and dedicated efforts of multiple Indian organizations, the changing of the laws may be accomplished but that is taking a long time and time we do not have to waste. There needs to be a grass roots, nationwide effort of all peoples of every race and color to join together to convince the politicians that the current status quo is unacceptable. Politicians are swayed by numbers; those numbers need to be tens of millions of constituents who are displeased with what is happening to the Indians in order to force changes in the legislation and bring about new enforceable laws. The Tea Party got its start when the masses of the silent majority got fed up with government. Perhaps there is a need for a new voice of the people to bring these demands to the Congress.

INTERNATIONAL EFFORTS

The Indian Trail Tree Project began a few short years ago in the United States with a few people from five states joining together to consolidate their combined efforts to save a part of the Indian cultural legacy. In a few years time, a lot of progress has been made and that process continues. Initially, the story of the Mystery of the Trees was confined to the southeastern and mid-western United States. Over time, that story not only grew to become a part of our nationwide history, it also grew in scope and depth to become a story that needs to be documented and made available to the public to educate them on this part of Native American history.

In researching this cultural and historical aspect of the Indigenous people's way of life, the scope of the story blossomed internationally expanding into Canada, Scandinavia, Australia, Turkey, New Zealand, some Asian countries and even Micronesia. Perhaps there is a need to develop an international effort to educate the public on this cultural aspect of Indigenous peoples world wide in order to preserve the artifacts and sacred places.

There is no end in sight to this story. With each day, new insights and new understandings are achieved as this very important aspect of the Indigenous people's way of life are discovered or rather re-discovered.

BIBLIOGRAPHY

1. Holton, Kerry. Chief of the Delaware Indians in Oklahoma filmed interview, June 2008.

2. Mooney, James. *Myths of the Cherokee, Nineteenth Annual Report of the Bureau of American Ethnology*, 1897-98.

3. Martorano, Marilyn. filmed interview at Florissant Fossil Bed National Monument in Florissant, Colorado, August 2008.

4. DeWeese, Dr. Georgina. filmed interview at the University of Tennessee Dendrochronology Laboratory, May 2007.

5. Grover, Frank R. *Our Indian Predecessors – The First Evanstonians*, A paper read before the Evanston Historical Society, November 2, 1901.

6. Grover, Frank R. *Some Indian Landmarks of the North Shore*, Chicago Historical Society, February 21, 1905

7. "Many North Shore Roads are Traced to Trails of Indians," *Wilmette Life Newspaper*, March 23, 1939.

8. *Indian Trail Markers*, Chicago newspaper, January 1955.

9. Silsbee, Margaret. *Trunks are Misshapen but Reason is Uncertained*, date unknown from Wilmette Public Library.

10. Wilmette newspaper, September 23, 1965.

11. Nicholson, Katherine Stanley. *Historic American Trees*, published by Frye Publishing Company, New York, 1922.

12. Janssen, Raymond E. "Indian Trail Markers," *Nature Magazine*, August 1938.

13. Janssen, Raymond E. "Living Guide-Posts of the Past," *Scientific Monthly*, Vol. 53, #1, July 1941.

14. Janssen, Raymond E. *Indian Trail Trees*, American Forests, July 1934.

15. From Wisconsin Department of Natural Resources, Ho- Chunk Department of Natural Resources

16. Allison, R. Bruce. *Every Root and Anchor, Wisconsin's Famous and Historic Trees*, published by the Wisconsin Society Press, 2005

17. Ritzerthaler, Robert E. "Trail Marker Trees," T*he Wisconsin Archeologist*, Vol. 46 #3, September 1965.

18. Maddux, Teresa. *Timber Talk, Bittersweet,* a publication of the Springfield-Green County Library, Volume VI, No. 2, Winter 1978.

19. Paschenko, Chris, "2006," *The Decatur Daily News*, July 24, 2006.

20. Red Eagle, Eddy interview at Osage Nation, August 2008.

21. Arum, Loya interview near Florissant, Colorado. August 2008.

22. Shaw, Billy interview near Huntsville, Alabama, October, 2007.

23. Smith-Rogers, Sheryl. "The Storytelling Place," *Texas Parks and Wildlife Magazine*, November 2006.

24. Toby Wells interview near Florissant, Colorado, August 2008.

25. Frizze, Shawn interview at Florissant Fossil Bed National Monument, Florissant, Colorado, August 2008.

26. Lewis, James interview in central Arkansas, July 2007.

27. Marshall, Lamar interview in Buckhead National Forest, August 2007.

28. "Travels in the Southlands, 1822-1823," *The Journal of Lucius Verus Bierce, Edited with Biographical Introduction by George W. Knepper*, Ohio State University Press, 1966.

29. "Letters of Benjamin Hawkins, 1796-1806," *Collections of the Georgia Historical Collections*, Vol. 9, Savannah, GA.

30. De Brahm, John Gerar William. *History of the Providence of Georgia*, Wormsloe, 1849.

31. Bartram, William. *Travels Through the North and South Carolina, Georgia, East and West Florida*, London, 1792.

32. "Placenames of Georgia," *Essay of John H. Goff, Edited by Francis Lee Utley and Marion R. Hemperly*, University of Georgia Press, Athens, 1975.

33. Fetherstonhaugh, George. *1837, Journal Account*, August 14, 1837.

34. Wade, Forest. *Cry of the Eagle*, self published in 1969.

35. Jordan, Elaine. *Indian Trail Trees*, Jordan Ink Publishing Company, Ellijay GA 1997.

36. Walker, Ricky Butch and Marshall, Lamar. *Indian Trails of the Warrior Mountains*, Lawrence Country Schools Education Program, Alabama State Council of the Arts, June 2005.

37. *Farmington (Missouri) Press* article from June 9, 1978.

38. Vickers, Kathryn. 1981, Farmington Press, March 25, 1981.

39. Thornton, Russell. *American Indian Holocaust and Survival: A Population History Since 1492*. University of Oklahoma Press, 1987.

40. Stannard, David E. *American Holocaust: Columbus and the Conquest of the New World*, Oxford University Press, 1992

41. Cook, Noble David. *Born to Die: Disease and the New World*

Conquest, 1492-1650. Cambridge: Cambridge University Press, 1998.

42. Rummel, R. J. *Death by Government, Chapter 3: Pre-Twentieth Century Democide,* New Brunswick, New Jersey. Transaction Publishers, 1991.

43. Koning, Hans. T*he Conquest of America: How the Indian Nations Lost Their Continent.* Monthly Review Press, 1993.

44. Churchill, Ward. *A Little Matter of Genocide: Holocaust and Denial in the Americas, 1492 to the Present.* City Lights Books, 1998.

45. Koning, Hans. op cit.

46. Churchill, Ward. op cit.

47. Stannard, David E. op cit.

48. Walker, Ricky Butch filmed interview 2008.

49. King, Gail, filmed interview 2009.

50. Goodin, Barbara interview at Comanche Nation, August 2008.

51. Jenkins, Ralph. *Cherokee Trail of Tears: Other Paths,* November 1996. 52.   Schoolcraft, Henry, *The American Indians, Their History, Conditions and Prospects,* George H. Derby and Co. Buffalo, New York, 1851.

53. Longfellow, Henry Wadsworth, *The Song of Hiawatha*, 1st Edition Tickner and Fields, Boston 1855.

54. U.S. Bureau of Ethnology Report, v. 7, pp. 149-299 by Walter James Hoffman, Washington, DC: Government Printing Office, 1891.

55. Mallery, Garrick, *Sign Language Among the North American Indians, Compared with that among Other peoples and Deaf-Mutes,* Smithsonian Institute – Bureau of Ethnology, 1881.

56. Ruxton, George Frederick Augustus, *Adventures in Mexico and the Rocky Mountains,* 1848.

57. Marshall, Lamar and Kathleen, *Wildsouth Magazine*, Winter 2007.

58. Belue, Ted Franklin, T*he Hunters of Kentucky: A Narrative History of American's First Far West, 1750-1779,* Stackpole Books, 2003.

59. Mooney, James, "Myths of the Cherokees," *Nineteenth Annual Report of the Bureau of American Ethnology* 1897-98, Part I. [1900].

60. Wade, Forest, *Cry of the Eagle*, published by Forest Wade, 1969.

61. Jackson, A.T. *Picture-Writing of Texas Indians,* The University; First Edition, 1938.

62. Getler, Warren and Brewer, Bob, *Rebel Gold*, published by Simon & Schuster Paperbacks, New York, NY 2003.

63. Goodin, Barbara. Comanche Language Program Historical Information.

64. Meyer, Jeff, "The Tree that Marked a Place in Our Past," *American Forests*, Autumn 2001.

65. Taylor, Anna Jean. *Searching for the Turning Trees and other Special Trees of the Comanche*, 1996.

66. Smith-Rodgers, Sheryl, "The Storytelling Place," *Texas Parks and Wildlife Magazine*, November 2006

67. Smits, David, "The Frontier Army and the Destruction of the Buffalo1865-1883," T*he Western Historical Quarterly*, 25 Autumn 1994, 313-339.

68. Wells, Toby, 2008 Filmed Interview Florrisant Colorado.

69. Kaelin, Celinda R., *Pikes Peak Backcountry*, Caxton Press Caldwell, Idaho, 1999

70. Kaelin, Celinda, *Ute Culturally Scarred Trees*, Pikes Peak Historical Society, 2003.

71. Ericsson, T.S., Ostlund, L., Andersson, R. *Destroying the Path to the Past – the Loss of Culturally Scarred Trees and Change in the Forest Structure along Allmunvagen, in Mid-West Boreal Sweden.* Silva Fennica 37(2): 283-298, 2003.

72. *The Providence of British Columbia, Culturally Modified Trees of British Columbia, A Handbook for the Identification and Recording of Culturally Modified Trees*, 2001.

73. Turner Nancy J., Ari, Yilmaz, Berkes, Fikret, Davidson-Hunt ,Iain, Ertug Z., Fusun and Miller, Andrew. "Cultural Management of Living Trees: An International Perspective," *Journal of Ethnobiology* 29(2): 237–270, 2009.

74. Dennison, Melissa. Ryerson University Canada. Report on internet.

75. Etheridge, R. & Geological Survey of New South Wales. *The Dendroglyphs or "Carved Trees" of New South Wales*, Dept. of Mines, Sydney, 1918.

76. Johnson-Gottesfeld, L.M. "The Importance of bark Products in the Aboriginal Economies of Northwestern British Columbia, Canada." *Economic Botany.* 46(2): 148-157. 1922.

77. Ostlund, Lars, Keane, Bob, Arno, Steve, Andersson, Rikard. "Culturally Scarred Trees in the Bob Marshall Wilderness, Montana, USA –Interpreting Native American Historical Forest Use in a Wilderness Area," *Native Areas Journal* 25(4) 315-325. 2005.

78. Martorano, Marilyn. 2008 Filmed interview at Florrisant Fossil Beds National Monument and personal communications.

79. Mobley, Charles, Lewis, Michael. "Tree-ring Analysis of Traditional Native Bark-Stripping at Ship Island, Southeastern Alaska, USA." *Vegetation History and Archaeobotany*, Vol.18 (3) 261-268,. 2009.

80. Mobley, Charles, Lewis, Michael, 1994. *Culturally Modified Trees at Bartlett Cove, Glacier Bay National Park, Alaska*, Archaeological Survey Report for the National Park Service.

81. Martorano, Marilyn A. *So Hungry They Ate the Bark Off a Tree.* Canyon Legacy 9:9-12. 1989.

82. Merrill, Marlin, 2008. Filmed interview at Eleven Mile State Park in Colorado.

83. *Curturally Modified Trees of British Columbia*, Archaeological Branch, British Columbia Ministry of Small Business, Tourism and Cluture. 2001.

84. Reddick, SuAnn, Colins, Gary. "Medicine Creek to Fox Island Cadastral Scams and Contested Domains," *Oregon Historical Quarterly*. Vol. 106 (3) Fall 2005

85. Mapes, Lynda. "After 153 Years, Treaty Tree Lost in Winter Storm," *Seattle Times* News Article, 2007.

86. Willard, Shirley, Cecrle, Judy, Fulton County Historical Society Quarterly Rochester Indiana No. 27, p. 21.

87. Johnson, Frederic, 1942 & 1949, *The Boylston Street Fish Weir*, Phillips Academy Foundation, Andover, Massachusetts.

88. Murphy, Gerald, *The Cleveland Free-Net*; Prepared by Nancy Troutman The Cleveland Free-Net; Distributed by the Cybercasting Services Division of the National Public Telecomputing Network (NPTN).

89. *Nineteenth Annual Report of the Bureau of American Ethnology,* Smithsonian Institute, July 1, 1898, Washington, DC.

90. Will, George, "Anthropological Papers of the American Museum of Natural History," *Archaeology of the Missouri Valley*, Vol. XXII, Part VI, American Museum Press, New York, 1924.

91. Jefferson, Thomas. *Notes on the State of Virginia,* J. W. Randolph, Richmond, Virginia 1853.

92. Stuart, David E. *Anasazi America: Seventeen Centuries on the Road from Center Place*, University of New Mexico Press, June 2000.

93. Lind, Neeta, "American Indian Sacred Places," *Native American Netroots*, December 2009.

94. Toensign, Gail Courney, *Passaconaway's Descendents Struggle to Protect Sacred Site*, September 2008.

95. Bushnell, David. "Native Cemeteries and Forms of Burial East of the Mississippi," *Bureau of American Ethnology Bulletin* 71; The Smithsonian Institution, 1920; p.11.

96. Rogers, Anne Frazer, "Fish Weirs as Part of the Cultural Landscape," *Appalachian Cultural Resources Workshop Papers*, Sept. 2008.

97. Frazier, Bill, personal communication.

98. Lutins, Allen. *Prehistoric Fishweirs in Eastern North America*, submitted as partial fulfillment of Masters Degree, State University of New York, Binghamton. 1992.

99. Rigby, J. Wilmer. *Lewis and Clark Expedition in Lemhi County,* Lemhi County Historical Committee.

100. Johnson, Becky, "Cherokee Youth Re-enact Ancient Fishing Practice," *Smokey Mountain News*, July 8, 2009.

101. Malone, James H. *The Chickasaw Nation, A Short Sketch of a Noble People,* John P. Morton & Company, Louisville, KY, 1922.

102. Featherstonbaugh, George W. *Journal Account of Travels through Cherokee Middle Towns*, 1837.

103. Belloe, Hilaire. *The Road* published in Manchester, UK, Charles W. Hobson, 1923.

104. Hemperley, Marion H. *Historic Indian Trails of Georgia, Atlanta:* Garden Club of Georgia, 1989.

105. Goff, John H., "Some Major Indian Trading Paths across the Georgia Piedmont," *Georgia Mineral News Letter* 6, no. 4 (1953): 122-31.

106. Myers, William E. "Indian Trails of the Southeast," in *Forty-second Annual Report of the Bureau of American Ethnology to the Secretary of the Smithsonian Institution,* 1924-25 (Washington, D.C.: U.S. Government Printing Office, 1928), 727-857.

107. Cherokee Nation v. State of Georgia, 30 US I, January Term 1831.

108. "Letters of Benjamin Hawkins 1796-1806," *Collections of the Georgia Historical Society,* Vol. IX , Savannah GA 1916.

109. French, Captain Christopher., *Journal of an Expedition to South Carolina, Journal of Cherokee Studies* (Summer 1977): 275-302.

110. Jaeger, Ellsworth. *Wildwood Wisdom*, Scribner, New York, 1945.

111. Ford, Bob. *Water Trails of the Anasazi,* published on the Internet, June 25 1997, Copyright Warlock Ink.

112. Dellenbaugh, Frederick , Powell, John, *A Canyon Voyage: The Narrative Of The Second Powell Expedition Down The Green-Colorado River From Wyoming, 1871-1872*, 1908.

113. Holton, Helen, *Black Beaver*, A Biography Unpublished

114. Harlan, Russell. "Lakota Sioux Secede From US, Declare Independence," *Rapid City Journal*, Dec. 21, 2007.

115. Sturgis, Sue. "Wal-Mart's History of Destroying Sacred Sites," *Institute of Southern Studies On-Line Magazine*, September 3, 2009.

116. Briefing to Congress, *Coalition to Protect Native American Sacred Places*, The Morning Star Institute, Washington, DC 2002.

ACKNOWLEDGEMENTS

Although this book was written by the authors, it could not have been done without the help of many people who collectively contributed to its completion. We are most grateful for their enthusiastic support of our efforts and their special insights that helped to open our eyes to this growing story that needed to be told.

Throughout our travels in researching this story, we encountered and interviewed elders from several Indian Nations who have taught us a great deal and helped us understand not only about the Indian Trees, The Indian Trails and the Indian way of life but more importantly about the impact on their culture from our ancestors. We can't name all that we met but the principal elders who assisted us were Kerry Holton, Chief of the Delaware Nation(Lenape) and his mother Helen Holton, a member of the Delaware Nation in Oklahoma, Eddy Red Eagle and Van Bighorse of the Osage Nation, Barbara Goodin and Billie Kreger of the Comanche Nation, Loya Arum of the Northern Ute Indian Nation, Jerry Wolfe of the Eastern Band of the Cherokee Indians and Thomas Belt of the Western Nation of the Cherokee Indians.

Along the way, we also had the pleasure of interviewing many "old timers," as they are often called, some who are of Indian descent who have special insights and family knowledge about parts of this story that they willingly shared which enriched our learning.

To fully develop this story we needed the help of the academic and historical community. Several members of that community provided expertise including Dr. Georgina DeWeese, a dendrochronologist; Marilyn Martorano, an archaeologist; Ricky Butch Walker, Past Director of the Oakville Indian Mounds Park and Museum; Gail King, Director Southeastern Anthropological Institute; Linda Pelon, McLennon Community College; Rick Wilson, Chief Park Ranger, Florissant Fossil Beds National Monument; Celinda Kaelin, Pikes Peak Historical Society; Luther Lyle and Dave LaVere, Oconee Art and Historical Commission; David Bogle, Museum of Native American Artifacts; and Andrew Miller, Natural Resources Institute, University of Manitoba, Winnipeg, Manitoba, Canada.

In many states across the nation, the effort has been supported by a large number of dedicated researchers. They have scoured the countryside looking for the "living artifacts" and related sites that are a legacy to the Native Americans' way of life. Their collective contribution is significant. Those who are researching the Indian Trails and locating them have also made a significant contribution.

In addition to the many people who monthly are researching trees and trails, there is a secondary group of people who have willingly searched their locales and submitted their findings through the Mountain Stewards web site. We can not begin to thank them for their interest and diligence.

There are a number of people who have provided financial assistance to the Trail Tree Project and we are grateful for their support. One in particular should be singled out for special recognition. Lynda Ramseur and the Lacy Foundation of Atlanta, GA, have contributed significant resources to this project over several years. Their philanthropic support made it possible for the Trail Tree Project to become a nationwide program is a few short years.

William Needs of Marietta, GA, contributed his time and talent in providing the illustrations in Chapter 4. We thank him for his support.

Janice Edens and John Edwards, who are experienced in book formatting and editing, provided their immense talents in doing the editing and initial formatted of the book into its early version. Dave Teffeteller, an expert in book preparation for printing provided untold hours getting the book into its final camera-ready copy format for printing. He also helped with finding printing companies to print the book and he is providing his expertise in marketing of the book. Without his help, this book would still be on the shelf.

Lastly, this story could not be told or this book written without the capability created by Google in Google Earth, Google Books, and Google search engines. Google has made it possible to bring together volumes of relational data to gain insights into a part of cultural history of the Native Americans that has long been out of sight and out of mind.

AUTHORS

DON WELLS

After completing a 28 year career in the US Navy Civil Engineer Corps and a ten year career in a private engineering consulting firm, Don and Diane retired to North Georgia in 2000 where they built their home as a Christian retreat center. In 2003, Don and several others formed the Mountain Stewards as a non-profit 501(c)(3) organization. Initially, the purpose of the organization was focused on developing hiking trails in North Georgia where none had previously existed. Their secondary purpose was locating and preserving Indian cultural heritage sites. In 2007, the Mountain Stewards launched, in conjunction with others, the National Trail Tree Project to locate, document and preserve Trail Trees which are part of the heritage of Native Americans. As a part of this project, the Mountain Stewards began developing a video documentary on the Trail Trees. In late 2007, the Mountain Stewards, in conjunction with WildSouth, Inc., launched the Indian Trails Mapping Program to more precisely map Indian Trails from old survey maps of the 1700 and 1800's era. Part of Don's heritage is Lenape Indian.

DIANE WELLS

Diane's career was is in education and history. She taught in the public school systems in places Don's Navy career took their family. With a passion for children who have trouble learning in crowded classrooms, she and her business partner set up a tutoring business to assist these children break out of the mold of being thought of as poor learners. Their tutoring business not only helped the children achieve academic successes but they helped the parents as well to mentor their children's continued success.

With a passion for history, she has been an integral part of the Indian Trail Tree Project serving in a research role and working in the field on mapping, filming and locating the Indian Trees. She is the co-author of the book Mystery of the Trees.

DR. JOHN (MICKEY) NARDO

Mickey is a retired physician specializing in Internal Medicine, Psychiatry, and Psychoanalysis. In addition to his medical background, he also has a background in mathematics and computers in a variety of capacities. In addition to teaching medicine at Emory University and having a private practice, he also taught computer courses. In the 1980's he wrote and sold software for managing offices of mental health professionals that is still in use today. He's now retired and describes himself as a "serial hobbyist." Part of his heritage is Cherokee Indian. Besides his interest in the trees themselves, what he brings to the team are computer skills for our trees, trail mapping, and Internet presence.

ROBERT WELLS

Since 1976, Robert has owned his own media production company and has produced photographic, audiovisual, film, video and printed materials for a wide variety of clients in government, medicine, education, manufacturing, real estate, financial services and broadcasting. He has filmed all over the United States and in Europe, Africa, Asia and South America, including documentary work in the Peruvian Amazon, Panama, China and Switzerland. Specializing in projects that include concept to completion, his current work includes high definition video production for Mountain Stewards, Inc., including oral histories and the documentary on Indian Trail Trees entitled Mystery of the Trees.

LAMAR MARSHALL

Lamar is the Cultural Heritage Director for Wild South, a non-profit conservation group with offices in Asheville and Cowee, NC and Moulton AL. Lamar is the founder of Wild South, 2003, formerly Wild Alabama, 1994. He served seventeen years as publisher and editor of Wild Alabama and Wild South Magazines. He was a co-founder of the Alabama Wilderness Alliance in 1993 whose mission is to preserve natural areas across the southeast. He is the co-author of the Wilderness Society's Alabama Mountain Treasures and Indian Trails of the Warrior Mountains. As a Board of Director member of the Alabama Chapter of the Trail of Tears Association, he mapped 200 miles of the 1838 Cherokee Removal Benge Detachment route which has been added to the National Historic Trail System. He is currently mapping the ancient Cherokee trail system across the southern Appalachians.

INDEX

H
Haida people 117-18
Hawkins, Benjamin 21, 160, 200, 204
hieroglyphics 87, 93
Ho-Chunk Nation 12-13
Holton, Kerry 1-2, 42, 129, 207
Hopewell Treaty 132
Hubler, Laura iii, 24, 31-2, 48, 52

I
Illinois 8, 10, 12, 137
Indian philosophy of life 129
Indian Removal Act 134
Indian Trail Tree Longevity Table 46
Indian Trail Tree Project 196, 212
Indian Trail Trees i-ii, 5, 8, 10, 14, 22, 31, 51, 144, 146, 200, 212
Indian Trails ii, 10, 13-14, 20, 22-4, 63, 65, 137, 140-1, 144, 146, 150, 156-60, 171-3, 194-5, 207-8
Indian Trails Mapping Program 156, 163-4, 211
Indian way of life v, 1-2, 4, 18-19, 33, 37, 42, 45, 129, 207
Indiana 13, 135
indigenous peoples 5, 34, 85, 111, 115-16, 122, 124, 127, 129, 139, 141, 149, 182, 187
Indigenous Symbology 85, 87, 89, 91, 93, 95, 97, 99
Iroquois 97-8, 115, 136

J
Jordan, Elaine i, iii, 22-3, 25
journal accounts 20, 22, 30, 200

K
Keowee Town 161, 174
Knight of the Golden Circle (KGC) 100

L
Lakota 183
Lenape Indians 130, 211
Lone Dog Winter Count 89
Longest Walk 181-2
longevity 45-6, 51, 109